## About the Author

Eduard Gracia has over twelve years of consulting experience, which he acquired throughout a variety of client engagements across the USA and Europe. He is currently based in London, where he works as a director at a global consultancy. He has been a lecturer of microeconomics at the University of Barcelona, and has published a number of papers on topics related to the ones covered in this book. His background also includes a degree in economics and an MBA.

# THE FABLE OF THE SHARKS

# POWER AND POLITICS IN TODAY'S BUSINESS ORGANISATIONS

## by

## *Eduard Gracia*

Published 2005 by arima publishing

www.arimapublishing.com

ISBN 1-84549-065-7

Printed and bound in the United Kingdom

Typeset in Verdana 9/12

arima publishing
ASK House, Northgate Avenue
Bury St Edmunds, Suffolk IP32 6BB
t: (+44) 01284 700321

www.arimapublishing.com

*To my parents,*
*without whose unwavering support*
*I would not have had the courage to write this.*

# CONTENT

# INTRODUCTION: THE FABLE OF THE SHARKS

*"Man is a wolf to man"* [1]

- Plautus, *Asinaria*

An old, remarkably persistent tradition depicts human society as a beehive. In this metaphor, the secret of both social and individual prosperity rests on teamwork, on a wise division of labour and a clear plan that everyone can follow. Under the right set of conditions, everyone from the queen to the last worker bee will conscientiously perform the role that has been allocated to her, and expect to receive her fair share of honey in return. The corridors of the happy colony will then resound with the serene buzz of myriads of laborious workers as they perform their toil.

Reality, alas, is not quite like this. Wherever two people work together, there is a potential for conflict; when there are hundreds or thousands in an organisation, the potential becomes a certainty. Anyone who has ever worked at a large corporation will recognise the picture. Managers abuse their power; subordinates shirk their duties; they all lie to protect themselves. Lies actually play an important role in this environment, because they sustain the fiction that everyone is on the same side –this is why it sometimes looks almost as if everyone conspired to turn deception into a way of life. Yet, *sotto voce*, the conflict subsists. Patently absurd decisions are made, or obvious ones fail to be made on time. Sensible strategies are not carried through, or end up being counterproductive, because they are not endowed with the right resources for their execution. People are too often rewarded for using bureaucratic obstruction to their advantage, for running away from disaster and taking credit for other people's successes, for manipulating their colleagues and schmoozing their way to the top... The end result of these activities is widespread waste at a huge scale: waste of time, of resources, of personal effort and goodwill.

When reading management literature, however, one often gets the impression that the parable of the beehive still shines bright in many of the authors' minds. For the most part, their ideas seem to imply that the difference between success and failure resides in the choice, communication and execution of the right strategy. Advice on what the "right" strategy actually entails in each case is not unanimous, to be sure, as the emphasis differs from author to author, is subject to the capricious winds of fashion and, ultimately, requires a difficult balance between the opposites: teamwork vs. individual contribution, strong leadership vs. empowerment, global thinking vs. local focus. There are also, to be fair, brilliant pieces about the power of the market's invisible hand, the difficulties of change management against entrenched interests or the potentially perverse effects of alternative incentive policies. Yet the one overarching idea that permeates most of this literature is still that the corporation is a body social whose illnesses can be cured with the right medicine. Just as it is for the patients of a physician, the first problem for these organisations is, according to this view, their ignorance of the sources of their pain and the remedies available to them. Hence, although they may not like the taste of the doctor's prescription, their will to heal is real, and convincing them to follow the instructions is thus simply a matter of persuading them, through honest and effective communication, that they are ultimately for their own good.

While I recognise there is some truth in this vision, after twelve long years in consulting I find it seriously difficult to accept as a fair representation of reality. True, at a detail level it is always possible to find cases where an innovative approach was enough to tackle a problem to everyone's satisfaction. Yet large corporate issues are very rarely left unresolved because of a lack of understanding of the potential solutions, but rather because the will to proceed with the changes required is missing precisely at the levels that hold the power to make them happen. It is due to these insidious dark forces that ambitious transformation efforts so frequently end up yielding no more than a few marginal improvements –much more frequently, in fact, than it is generally acknowledged, for many of the "success stories" that fill management books look a lot less impressive when analysed in detail. All human organisations suffer this split personality syndrome to a greater or lesser extent: they are associations of individuals in pursuit of the common good, but at the same time they are also political swamps of internal conflict.

Against the fable of the beehive, I would thus propose that of a fish school –but we have to imagine it composed of many different types of fish, some small peaceful sardines, some large bloodthirsty sharks, but most of them somewhere in the middle and able to play one role or the other depending on the circumstances. Larger sharks eat smaller sharks, and are eaten in turn by even larger ones –while those at the bottom of the food chain feed on tasteless plankton. It is convenience, not team spirit, what brings the fish together into a single formation, and what makes them swim in seemingly perfect coordination, instantly reacting to changes in the water current, just as human organisations are shaken by the invisible hand of the market. Seen from the outside, the overall fish community could appear irrationally inefficient, as sharks devote their energies to chasing other fish while their potential victims spend most of their efforts trying to avoid being caught. Yet there is nothing irrational in it: as long as an individual fish is better off as a shark than as a sardine, there will be no point in trying to persuade it that it would be much better for everyone else if it went back to peacefully feeding on plankton just as other, smaller fish do.

This representation of social hierarchy as a food chain where those at the bottom of the pyramid have to work to feed not only themselves but also the predators (i.e., the chiefs) above them is, as it happens, probably even older than that of the beehive. Egyptian pharaohs portrayed themselves as sphinxes with a human head on the body of a lion; American Indian chiefs decorated their headgear with eagle feathers; African kings covered their bodies with lion or leopard skins. Power symbols in our times have become more subtle and less animalistic –like the shoulder padding of business suits, which makes their carrier look more broad-shouldered, or the raised fist that symbolises allegiance to left-wing associations– but the underlying message is still the same. To the extent wielding power implies the capability to exploit the weaker, and to the extent this same power is required to restrict internal depredation and move towards a more efficient organisation, the weight of political inertia against any such well-meaning endeavours will always be very heavy –and sometimes fatal.

This book is about the dynamics of power in large organisations, the disguises it adopts and the damage it causes. There is a widespread belief that office politics are as unavoidable a cost of team work as friction in a mechanical engine. This is no doubt true –but, just like friction in an engine, office politics can go, depending on the surrounding conditions, from being a tolerable nuisance to grinding the whole system to a halt. We are not going to change human nature –and we ignore it at our peril. Instead of dismissing these unpleasant realities as "inertia" or as "communication issues", we need to analyse them carefully if we want to minimise their damage. *For office politics are not a known, constant quantity: there are sets of conditions that minimise them and others that make them grow like a cancer until they bring the whole enterprise to its knees.*

The aim of this book is to make a contribution to our understanding of these conditions. It does not intend to be a cookbook –as a matter of fact, I very much doubt that attempting to write such a book would constitute a worthwhile or even sensible exercise. Management fads have such a poor reputation precisely because they try to give simple answers to complex questions: this is why they are the snake oil of economics. In reality, individual solutions need to be tailored to individual problems; yet to do so one needs to understand first the overall rules of the game. I hope this book will throw a bit more light on some of these rules.

There is now an intense sense of urgency around this topic. For the last thirty years or so, the corporate world in most developed countries has suffered a number of dramatic changes that some do not hesitate to describe as an "Organisational Revolution" [2] comparable to the Industrial Revolution that started over two centuries ago. In the process, however, there is significant evidence that office politics at many large organisations have become, if anything, even more insidious and widespread. The very fact that *Dilbert*, perhaps the first wide-circulation comic strip ever to focus on office politics and the absurdities of corporate life, has become such a wild success in the last twenty years strongly suggests that something is not quite right, and that people are now more concerned about it than their parents used to be.

In the midst of turbulent change, conflicts of interests and attempts to preserve old privileges at all cost frequently result in organisations sailing straight into their worst nightmare. In the aftermath of the largest financial bubble in recorded history, under the heat of street protests against globalisation and job offshoring, there is still today a tendency to recommend solutions that assume the underlying issue to be sheer ignorance instead of a conflict of interests –see, for example, the numerous recent calls for a strengthening of ethics training in the MBA curriculum. If we think dysfunctional organisations are like beehives where the bees somehow got their roles confused, this type of remedy may indeed be the answer; but if they are like our school of opportunistic sharks, then it is as likely to be effective as an aspirin would be to cure a brain tumour.

# 1. THE AGE OF SPEED

*"Now, here, you see, it takes all the running you can do to keep in the same place. If you want to get somewhere else, you must run at least twice as fast as that!"*

- Lewis Carroll, *Through the Looking Glass*

On 17 February 1570, Tsar Ivan the Terrible rode across the gates of the city of Pskov, surrounded by his personal guard –the fearful *opritchniki*, ominously dressed in black. Only a few days before he had left neighbouring Novgorod where, in an orgy of death that had lasted well over a month, he had all but exterminated the inhabitants of the city –many thousands of men, women and children, whom he accused of conspiracy against him. His blood thirst not yet satiated, now he intended to inflict the same punishment on Pskov. The terrified citizens placed small tables with offerings of bread and salt in front of their homes, and prostrated themselves on the snowy ground as a sign of submission. One man, however, stood up to the Tsar: Nikolai the hermit, a holy fool, standing semi-naked in the middle of the Russian winter and carrying heavy chains around his neck as a sign of penitence, extended his hand to offer a piece of raw meat to the monarch. "I am a Christian and do not eat meat during Lent" retorted he, confused. To this the anchorite replied: "you do worse: you feed on human flesh and blood, forgetting not only Lent but God himself" – and then threatened him with heavenly punishment if he all but hurt even the smallest of the children of Pskov. According to the Russian chronicles, a thunder rolled then in the distance, fear seized the heart of the Tsar, and the city was saved.

Holy fools rarely make such spectacular interventions in our days, nor do they usually need to display so much personal courage under our modern, democratic regimes –but this does not mean their role is any less necessary. It will always take a fool or a child to point out aloud that the Emperor has no clothes. In these our less religious times, however, these warnings are no longer delivered amid the wrathful indictments of a prophet but rather as the sarcastic jokes of a clown. So it was that, in the mid-20th Century, Schultz's *Charlie Brown* comic strips expressed the secret anguish of a growing community of American suburbanites for whom perpetual extroversion and finely-tuned social skills seemed (and still seem) to be life's number one requirement. And so it is now that Scott Adam's *Dilbert* cartoons express the real issues of today's white collar workplace much better than any of our contemporary management books.

*Dilbert* is perhaps the most spectacular editorial success of the last fifteen or twenty years. According to the official website, Scott Adams' comic strips are regularly published in over 2,000 newspapers across 65 countries, while his management books have appeared many times at the top of the annual best-selling lists. Every year, millions of Dilbert calendars are sold, and their proud owners display them on their office desks; often, they enjoy a particular comic strip so much that they stick it on the walls of their cubicles, or photocopy it and pass it around to their colleagues with a grin of complicity. When we ask the fans themselves, what they seem to enjoy most is how Dilbert satirises the absurd situations caused by bureaucracy, politics and power-mongering in large corporations which they routinely experience as part of their daily working lives. In other words, as in any good satire, the punch of these cartoons is not in the joke itself but in the bit of truth that hides behind it –for there is often more truth in the words of a fool than in those of the prudent and the wise.

The first and probably best known of Adams' books, *The Dilbert Principle*, summarised its core thesis as follows:

> "Stories like these prompted me to do the first annual Dilbert Survey to find out what management practices were most annoying to employees. The choices included the usual

suspects: Quality, Empowerment, Reengineering and the like. But the number-one vote-getter in this highly unscientific survey was 'Idiots Promoted to Management.'"

"This seemed like a subtle change from the old concept by which capable workers were promoted until they reached their level of incompetence –best described as the 'Peter Principle'. Now, apparently, the incompetent workers are promoted directly to management without ever passing through the temporary competence stage."[3]

These statements are of course sarcastic, but for anyone with first-hand experience in large organisations it is tempting to follow Adams' lead and claim that they are run by incompetents who systematically single-out other incompetents for the faster career track. Yet upon further reflection it is almost equally easy to realise that this is very seldom, if ever, the case. Instead, the strong impression one gets when working with large corporations is one of capable and often very intelligent individuals immersed in environments that seem purposefully designed to generate highly inefficient, even self-defeating behaviours.

Taken at face value, this seems a far cry from the world of classical economics where private corporations are above all profit-maximising entities –but at the same time it is not a world of irrational individuals either. This Dilbert world is a closer relative of *Alice in Wonderland*'s or of Kafka's *The Process*, a world where rational human beings are held in perpetual bafflement by the apparent nonsense of the rules that govern their environment, and where, by trying to adapt, they end up behaving just as absurdly as everyone else around them. To a large extent, this is old news –in fact, although the inefficiencies associated to hierarchical organisations are not easy to quantify in pounds and pence, they are a well-known phenomenon whose existence and relevance few economists would question[4]. Yet Scott Adams' assertions also carry a time-related component, for they suggest that a change has taken place throughout the last few decades in the way management positions are awarded –a change that, he seems to imply, has been for the worse. In truth, this sort of statement smells a bit too much like good old nostalgia for an idealised past: after all, the inefficiencies of hierarchy are by no means a new phenomenon. So, should we simply dismiss Scott Adams' statements as witticisms supported only by popular prejudice?

Not so fast. While not everyone agrees on its causes and nature, there is strong evidence suggesting that the last three or four decades *have* indeed seen a significant change in the structure of corporate organisations at most developed countries, and that this change has permeated through all dimensions of the body social. Michael Jensen, the pioneer of modern organisation theory, goes so far as to state that "we have not seen such a metamorphosis of the economic landscape since the Industrial Revolution in the nineteenth century."[5] Sociological research has also taken note of this new state of things, and some authors have coined rather eloquent terms to describe it: Richard Sennett[6] calls it "flexible capitalism"; Zygmunt Bauman [7] , "liquid modernity"; Ulrich Beck [8] , "the risk society". Management literature has ranted *ad nauseam* about the fast-changing, intensely competitive, increasingly global nature of the contemporary marketplace. Corporate speakers confirm the prognosis just as forcefully as they emphasise the need for "flexibility", "instant response" and a willingness to "embrace change"... Somehow, thus, both supporters and detractors of the new order seem to agree that the world of work has become more fluid, fast-paced and unpredictable.

Not that this should come as a surprise. It is already a commonplace that competition has become much more intense in the last thirty years. The change has perhaps been most evident in America, for the USA has been, in this as in so many other social changes throughout the last two centuries, at the forefront of the developed world. In the U.S., the alarm bell started to ring in the late 1960s and early 1970s with the realisation that the American industrial machine no longer ruled the world. The U.S. corporations had benefited, in the aftermath of World War II, from the attenuated competitive climate that came with the destruction of the industrial infrastructures of Europe and Japan. In 1967 it was still possible for French journalist Jean-Jacques Servan-Schreiber to argue convincingly, in his bestseller *Le Défi Américain* * that Western Europe's inferior industrial power would lead it to become a mere branch office for American multinationals[9]. By 1971, however, the competitiveness gap of the U.S. economy against its main trading partners had become so wide that President Nixon had to suspend the dollar gold convertibility and let the greenback dive in the currency markets. Competition had intensified; nothing could be taken from granted anymore. From an economic policy perspective, after a long period of soul-searching and political confrontation in the seventies, the solution was to move away from the interventionism of the forties, deregulate and increasingly let the market take care of itself –the eighties were, after all, the days of Ronald Reagan and Margaret Thatcher. State companies were privatised, monopolies abolished, the power of unions curbed… As liberalisation gained momentum, it gradually extended like an oil spot over the world map. It took a bit longer for the change to take hold in Continental Europe and Japan, and the process there is still comparatively behind the curve. Yet, at variable speeds, the whole community of developed countries is essentially sliding in the same direction. And not only developed countries: China started liberalising in the mid-eighties, the Communist Eastern Block around the USSR dissolved in the early nineties and now India, traditionally a heavily interventionist country, seems to have become the offshoring location of choice for the early 21st Century.

*****

A competitive world is by definition an uncertain world: if I compete against my neighbour for a prize, it cannot be known beforehand who of us is going to win –or else one of us would just not bother and quit the game. It is also, on the same token, a world of inequality: after the race, one of us will end up with a prize and the

---

* *The American Challenge*

other one will not. If the players start from radically different positions there is always a possibility that the least privileged win more of the prizes and, as a result, overall inequality be reduced. Yet, to the extent the starting positions are fairly even, a more intensely competitive environment can only end up increasing the dispersion of incomes. This is exactly what has happened. Particularly in the USA and, to a lesser extent, the U.K., overall income inequality, which had been remarkably stable since the end of World War II, started in the early 1970s to drift upwards, slowly at first and then, from the 1980s onwards, at a faster pace[10] (although in the U.K. this process appears to have somewhat slowed down again from 1990 onwards). In the event, educated workers came out better off than uneducated ones: in the U.S., the average real salary earnings of college graduates rose by 5% between 1979 and 1994, while those of high school graduates declined by 20% throughout the same period[11].

Maybe even more significantly, at least half of the rise in earnings inequality in the U.S. took place within groups, as defined by observable traits such as education, experience, occupation, race and gender[12], and about a third of this was due to greater volatility of earnings[13]. A remarkable paper by Raghuram Rajan and Julia Wulf [14], after analysing data from 300 large U.S. corporations between 1986 and 1999, concluded that "pay and long-term incentives are becoming more like in a partnership", i.e., with steeper compensation differentials between one level and the next, and a larger variable component of the overall pay. In short: the earnings gap marking the difference between career success and failure has become a lot wider. As we move up the hierarchy to celebrity-CEO levels, these differentials reach magnitudes that are nothing short of spectacular. Another researcher, Kevin Murphy[15], found that the average S&P 500 CEO made 30 times more than the average production worker in 1970, but that this ratio had climbed to 140 times by 1991 and to 210 times by 1996... and the trend apparently did not stop there for, as *Fortune* magazine[16] recently pointed out, the ratio for 2003 was already close to 500 times (!).

There is a widespread fallacy according to which new technologies explain why organisation structures have changed and why the "education premium" (i.e., the difference between the average weekly earnings of college graduates and those of a high school graduates) had increased, at least in the USA. Technology can be used as readily to support centralisation as the opposite –as a matter of fact, the same argument of technological progress driving organisation change is frequently used to explain the massive industrial consolidation of the late 19th Century. Indeed, as we will see in Chapter 6, technology in Frederick Taylor's days enabled firms to pursue levels of centralisation that would previously have been unthinkable. Daniel Bell, in a classical study of the General Motors Willow Run plant in Michigan in the 1950s, noted that the "superstructure which organizes and directs production [...] draws all possible brainwork away from the shop; everything is centered in the planning and schedule and design departments"[17]. Modern information technology is not any different. For instance, in the days of our grandparents, shopkeepers had to be able to add up by hand long lists of numbers quickly and accurately while their customers waited. Twenty years ago, they still had to be able to read a price tag and key it into a cash register machine. Today, all they need to do is to pass the bar coded tag through a reading machine and push a button to produce the result. Hence, at modern supermarkets, it is not manpower as much as brainpower what is being saved by centralising all intellectual activity on the small team that maintains the computer system.

The fact is that technology can result in reduced as well as enhanced education requirements for a given job. So it is not the "knowledge economy" per se what imposes the need for "brainwork" to take place at all levels in the organisation. It is when the process cannot be so perfectly integrated, when it requires more flexibility than rigorous planning can provide, that it becomes necessary to spread the "brainwork" down the hierarchy together with the responsibility for meeting preset objectives. It is of course also true that more powerful communications technology allows providers from cheaper locations to compete on a level ground with the local producers. But this in only happening because the incumbent countries have at the same time decided to liberalise their economies. For example, European corporations are today much more likely to offshore their operations to East Asia than to North Africa, which is geographically much closer, simply because the legal framework in Morocco, Algeria or Tunisia is a lot less favourable to business. In short, the causal arrow goes in the opposite direction: market pressure drives organisation change, and organisation change drives demand for a technology to support it. Technology enables, but does not explain organisation change: the market does.

In any event, the world has changed —and it would have been odd indeed if the new environment had not triggered a parallel transformation in the way firms were run. Under the pressure of the market's invisible hand, corporate leadership styles just had to adapt —but in what direction, and with what results?

## 2.  MANAGEMENT STYLES OLD AND NEW

> *"For all his inner suffering, the narcissist has many traits that make for success in bureaucratic institutions, which put a premium on the manipulation of interpersonal relations, discourage the formation of deep personal attachments and at the same time provide the narcissist with the approval he needs in order to validate his self-esteem."*
>
> - Christopher Lasch, *The Culture of Narcissism*

In 1981, when the world was at the deep end of the so-called Second Oil Crisis, Marvin Harris, the American anthropologist, published a short essay titled *America Now: the Anthropology of a Changing Culture*[18]. In it, he analysed the economic phenomena underlying the wide cultural change that had been observed since the late 1960s and early 1970s. His argument was that these changes could to a large extent be traced back to the general lack of reliability of goods and services produced in the U.S. at that time, and that this, in turn, was attributable to the short-term-oriented management style that dominated corporate America:

> "Insiders agree that there is something very different in the way today's executives relate to their corporations which sets them apart from an earlier generation of business leaders. [...] Large corporations have been virtually overrun by a proliferation of MBAs [...] who are trained to tighten every operation to get 'good quarterly results' and who have little interest in the effects of their activities several years hence. By then they hope to have been hired by another conglomerate."

Nothing is new under the sun. Already a quarter of a century ago, numerous voices, including Harris', were raised against the "myopia" of a corporate system that was willing to reward short-term performance at the expense of long-term viability –and were more or less as ineffective then as they have been for the last few years. Not even executive pay scandals are new: in 1981, for example, when Harris' book was still hot off the press, scandal hit the news as Roger Smith, then CEO of General Motors, awarded himself a US$ 1.5 million bonus in the midst of the severest recession the U.S. automobile industry had ever experienced[19].

This "new" management style was as much of a child of the late sixties as any of the other structural changes we described in the preceding chapter. It was precisely in 1971 when Eugene Emerson Jennings heralded, in his classical *Routes to the Executive Suite*, the demise of the 1950's "organization man" and the dawn of a new "era of mobility" at the executive ranks[20]. With over thirty years behind its back, one can hardly describe this as a "new" phenomenon any more. If anything, the feeling of novelty is justified by its very success, as it expands and intensifies beyond its social and geographical origins and therefore may appear to be "different", in the sense of larger and more deeply rooted, every time one looks at it again. Indeed, the flexibility and interpersonal skills that in the 1970s were increasingly demanded from executives now seems to be expected from virtually everyone at all levels in the corporate organisation.

Jennings was quite categorical in announcing that "the self-sacrificing company man" had become "an obvious anachronism", but the fact is that, in many aspects, there was continuity rather than rupture. Just as in the case of the organisation man that preceded him in the 1950s, or of the members of any other bureaucratic élite (think, for example, of the Imperial Russian bureaucrats whose lives Tolstoy portrayed so sharply in his *Death of Ivan Ilych*), what matters most for the contemporary manager's prospects of career advancement are his social and networking skills, even at the expense of "objective" performance. There is absolutely no difference between the unwritten rule of "never say anything controversial" that William Whyte[21] found to be key to managerial success in his 1956 classic *The Organization Man* and the "ability to say almost anything without antagonising others" that Jennings identified as equally critical in his 1971 book, nor between the latter and our contemporary obsession with political correctness. Richard Sennett, for instance, draws the following conclusion from the experiences of one of his interviewees at an advertising agency in New York:

> "The successful people in the advertising business are not necessarily the most ambitious, since everyone is driven. The really successful ones seem the most adept at walking away from disaster, leaving others to hold the bag; success consists in avoiding the reckonings of the accountant's bottom line. 'The trick is, let nothing stick to you.' To be sure, there is in every enterprise in the end a bottom line. What struck Rose was that, even after such a reckoning, a person's past record of failures counted for less than contacts and networking skills."

Whether we like the attitude of this type of corporate animal or not, the fact is that he (or she) is, in this sense, no less of an "organisation man" than before. Ivan Ilych would smile knowingly.

Yet he lives in a much more dangerous world now –a world where it is much more vital not to be the one left holding the bag. He cannot count on the corporation to shelter him against the capricious winds of the outside world any more, because these have become too powerful for any organisation to resist for any significant length of time. As a consequence, he cannot entrust his career to his organisation either –he needs to "keep his options open". Long before the downsizing era, Jennings could already quote a professor of management according to whom "overidentification" with the company "produces a corporation with enormous power over the careers and destinies of its true believers" and who therefore advised executives "to manage their careers in terms of their own [...] free choices" and to "maintain the widest set of options possible." This may have sounded a bit cynical in 1971 but, after the impact of the corporate downsizing waves of the 1980s and early 90s on the American middle management ranks, it has become pure common sense. Indeed, and this must be said to their credit, many companies have decided to openly recognise the new state of affaires and explicitly give the same type of advice to their employees. In the words of Andrew Grove, Chairman and CEO of Intel:[22]

> "The sad news is, nobody owes you a career. Your career is literally your business. You own it as a sole proprietor. You have one employee: yourself. You are in competition with millions of businesses: millions of other employees all over the world. You need to accept ownership of your career, your skills and the timing of your moves. It is your responsibility to protect this personal business of yours from harm and to position it to benefit from the changes in the environment. Nobody else can do that for you."

To be sure, this sort of statement is typically made aloud only in self-confident businesses that offer enough variety of opportunities to expect those "career opportunities" to be found more often than not within the same organisation –but the advice is just as valid, if not more, for companies that do not feel strong enough to make the point so blatantly explicit to their people.

Perhaps more revealingly still, this attitude of detachment has also spread down the hierarchy to the shop floor level in the years since. At around the time Jennings published his book on executive careers, Jonathan Cobb and Richard Sennett were conducting the research on blue-collar workers whose results they published in their 1972 book, *The Hidden Injuries of Class*. Among other aspects of the American work landscape, this study described a generalised pattern of long-term employment and craft pride, which in some cases was even passed over to the next generation –for example at a certain Boston bakery where the employees, most of them of Greek descent, had spent nearly all their working lives at the same job. A quarter of a century thereafter, when Sennett went back to visit the same bakery, he found a very different picture: a highly automated shop floor operated by temporary, non-specialised workers (incidentally, none of them Greek) who were all looking at their job as just an interim stage that should last only until such time as they would find an opportunity to jump ship and switch to a more promising occupation.

Yet we started this chapter with Marvin Harris' accusing finger pointed towards short-term thinking as the most damaging characteristic of this new managerial character, so we might as well ask ourselves: how justified is this charge?

If short-term management thinking means making decisions solely on the basis of their foreseeable outcomes within a short timeframe, then it should not be a surprise that, under increased competitive pressure, executives simply can afford less waiting time until the benefits of their decisions mature. Indeed, the length of average tenure at corporate leadership positions has gradually but consistently eroded over the last quarter of a century –slowly at first, faster in the most recent times. For example, Rakesh Khurana[23], after examining 1,300 occasions between 1980 and 1996 in which chief executives of *Fortune 500* firms left their jobs, found that, for similar levels of performance, a chief executive appointed after 1985 was three times as likely to be fired as one appointed before that date. That this tendency has become even more pronounced after 1996 is confirmed in a more recent study[24] based on a sample of 2,500 big publicly traded companies worldwide. According to this paper, even if we dismiss the executive turnover of 2001 and 2002 as due to the several sharp stock market declines that took place after November 2000, the global incidence of performance-related CEO turnover in large firms went up from 1.0% in 1995 to 3.2% in 2000. Most spectacularly, in the specific case of the U.S.A., this ratio went from 1.3% to 5.2% throughout the same years –i.e., a fourfold increase in scarcely five years. European companies, although still somewhat less "trigger-happy", followed a similar path over this period, climbing from 1.0% CEO turnover in 1995 to 2.7% in 2000. Furthermore, the same study also points out that the average tenure of CEOs that were replaced for performance-driven reasons went down dramatically from 7 years in 1995 to 4.8 in 2000 and, in the case of the U.S., from 8.9 years in 1995 to 4.9 in 2000 –in other words, in only five years the average timeframe within which an executive is expected to deliver results has reduced to just a bit over half of what it used to be. Yes, the organisation man of our times may still be a bureaucrat, but he is now a bureaucrat with a sense of urgency.

How does this impact the corporate decision-making process? Both the classic economic argument in defence of free market competition and the strong case business literature has been making for decades in favour of management by measurable objectives are well known enough –but the evidence from the recent corporate scandals now seems to challenge this doctrine. The aggressive culture of internal competition at Enron, for example, has repeatedly been highlighted as a key element that contributed to the company's spectacular failure[25]. Informally known among the staff as "rank and yank", the Enron annual performance reviews, which typically resulted in the bottom 10% performers being fired, fostered an environment where, in the words of a former employee, "people went from being geniuses to idiots overnight". The result was Enron's famous "laser-focus" on earnings per share, no doubt, but also a culture where people, according to another insider, "were so goal-oriented toward immediate gratification that they lost sight of the future". Nonetheless, before its spectacular collapse in late 2001, Enron had been awarded *Fortune* magazine's sobriquet of "the most innovative firm in America" for six consecutive years, and was widely regarded as an outstanding showpiece of corporate excellence. Furthermore, the "rank and yank" policy had been borrowed straight from General Electric, one of today's most admired companies, where this aggressive approach to human resource management has been in place since the 1980s. So when journalist Malcolm Gladwell echoed general sentiment by asking in *The New Yorker* magazine: "what if Enron failed not in spite of its talent mindset but because of it?"[26], he was indeed posing an unsettling question. The suspicion is not that the waves of corporate failures were due to any sudden seizure of general stupidity, but to the fact that, in Zygmunt Bauman's words, "'Rational choice' in the era of instantaneity means to pursue gratification while avoiding the consequences, and particularly the responsibilities which such consequences may imply." Or, as Richard Sennett puts it[27]:

> "The work ethic, as we commonly understand it, asserts self-disciplined use of one's time and the value of delayed gratification. [...] Such a work ethic depends in part on institutions stable enough for a person to practice delay. Delayed gratification loses its value, though, in a regime whose institutions change rapidly; it becomes absurd to work long and hard for an employer whose thinks only about selling up and moving on."

The argument is clear, forceful and largely supported by the evidence available. Nevertheless, when one considers it in the light of a longer historical perspective, it is difficult not to reach the conclusion that, while these statements doubtlessly contain a good deal of truth, they probably do not reflect the whole truth. After all, this heavier stress on the market's sovereign power represents, in many respects, a return to the conditions of the earlier stages of industrialisation. Indeed, when in the late 1940s and early 50s the bureaucratic, socially-proficient, "grey-flannel-suit" man committed to a lifetime career within the corporation was identified in America as a new human subspecies, he was not precisely hailed with enthusiasm. Despite their avowed intention of presenting the facts under an impartial light, most contemporary observers could not help expressing their concern about the disappearance, in this new managerial persona, of the aggressively competitive, entrepreneurial traits that had characterised the businessmen of the previous generation. David Riesman[28], for instance, described the change as a process through which the "invisible hand" of free market was gradually being replaced by the "glad hand" of the welfare society. In the same context, William Whyte noted that the new system put the "emphasis on cooperation rather than competition" and that the old regime of "survival of the fittest" that dominated the first stages of industrialisation had been replaced with one where "while there may be promotion of the fittest, there can be survival for all." Whyte was particularly concerned that this mild-mannered "social ethic", so different from the ruthless individualism of early American capitalism, would breed conformity, mediocrity and ultimately stagnation in the long run.

So, if the rule of survival of the fittest is back, does it mean that we are returning to the world of the great captains of industry and the "robber barons" (who, we should never forget, were often the same people)? If so, then something does not feel quite right: first, because the ways of our world of political correctness are light-years apart from the straightforward ruthlessness of those days and, second, because the industry captains of old were in many respects as short-term-focused as one could possibly be –at least according to our modern standards. For instance, in one of the unforgettable anecdotes of his book, Whyte describes vividly how the core message of early American capitalism was delivered to the trainees at the Vicks School of Applied Merchandising (among whom he counted himself) in 1939:

> "Shortly before we were to set out from New York, the president, Mr. H. S. Richardson, took us up to the Cloud Club atop the Chrysler Building. The symbolism did not escape us. As we looked from this executive eyrie down on the skyscraper spires below, Golconda stretched out before us. One day, we gathered, some of us would be coming back up again –and not as temporary guests either. Some would not. The race would be to the swiftest."

> "Over coffee Mr. Richardson drove home to us the kind of philosophy that would get us back up. He posed a hypothetical problem. Suppose, he said, that you are a manufacturer and for years a small firm has been making paper cartons for your product. He has specialized so much to service you, as a matter of fact, that that's all he does make. He is utterly dependent on your business. For years the relationship has continued to be eminently satisfactory to both parties. But then one day another man walks in and says he will make the boxes for you cheaper. What do you do?"

> "He bade each one of us in turn to answer."

"But *how much* cheaper? we asked. How much time could we give the old supplier to match the new bid? Mr. Richardson became impatient. There was only one decision. Either you were a businessman or you were not a businessman. The new man, obviously, should get the contract. Mr. Richardson, who had strong views on the necessity of holding to the old American virtues, advised us emphatically against letting sentimentality obscure fundamentals. Business was survival of the fittest, he indicated, and we would soon learn the fact."

This is shark-like behaviour of the worst kind, and there is no doubt it would attract today the most heated indictments against its lack of long-term focus. Yet, however much we may dislike their methods, these unscrupulous entrepreneurs founded corporate empires that have survived for generations after their deaths and, for the most part, still dominate the economic landscape of today. In fact, when Whyte included this personal anecdote in his book, he explicitly did so to provide an example of the robust business attitude that, he thought, ought to be given much of the credit for America's early entrepreneurial success, and whose gradual mellowing he regarded as a serious concern. It is difficult to challenge his point. Vicks itself, after all, managed to thrive in the cutthroat market of low-tech, over-the-counter pharmaceuticals, and grew to become one of the leaders of the sector –and, what is more, did so largely on the basis of the success of a product as basic as the famous VapoRub. We can accuse those ruthless entrepreneurs of lacking scruples, for sure, but we cannot seriously accuse them of lacking a long-term vision.

Does this contradict the assertions we have quoted from Harris, Sennett and Bauman? I do not think so –but it suggests that their analysis is somewhat incomplete. In the next chapters we will see why.

# 3.  WINNER-TAKE-ALL GAMES

> *"It is not from the benevolence of the butcher, the brewer, or the baker, that we expect our dinner, but from their regard to their own interest. We address ourselves, not to their humanity, but to their self-love, and never talk to them of our necessities but of their advantages."*
>
> - Adam Smith, *The Wealth of Nations*

> *"Hereby it is manifest that, during the time men live without a common power to keep them all in awe, they are in that condition which is called war; and such a war, as is of every man against every man."*
>
> - Thomas Hobbes *Leviathan*

Imagine a country with, say, ten cities, in each one of which lives a single doctor, and let us also assume there are strong limitations for people to go visit physicians in cities other than their own, be it due to a deficient transport system, to a legal system that requires them to resort to a local doctor, or to any other reason. The income of each one of the physicians, assuming the size and morbidity of the different cities to be roughly the same, will thus also tend to be more or less alike. The physicians, under these conditions, will not have many incentives to invest in advertising themselves, as there is no pressure for competition, and the control by each one of them of his/her own city market will have monopolistic characteristics, with the corresponding impact on price and quality. On the other hand, the investment planning horizon of each one of the physicians will tend to be relatively long, as the expectation is that each city market will belong to its local doctor for a long time, and perhaps even pass to his or her descendants.

Now suppose that the barriers to free competition disappear: communications improve between the cities, and there are no legal restrictions to prevent people from freely choosing any doctor. What happens now? To begin with, of course, customers will tend to go to the doctor with the best reputation. Thus, other things being equal, the income of the best physicians will rise, and that of the worst will decline. At the extreme (e.g., if the best physician can really deal with all the patients and all the other doctors end up with no business), this is just a winner-take-all game. There will be competitive pressure both on prices and quality and on the proportion of their income the physicians spend on advertising themselves. There will also be a strong tendency for success (or failure) to retro-feed itself: the most successful doctors will make more money and, therefore, be able to afford both better equipment and more expensive advertising. This means that winning in the next few rounds of the game has a potentially very high relevance, as it determines to a large extent the conditions under which the player is going to have to compete afterwards. Yet success will always have the potential of being short-lived, because tomorrow an unfortunate mistake in a difficult surgery procedure or the appearance of a new, better advertised or genuinely more gifted competitor can trigger the vicious cycle of failure for the physician that today is at the top of the world. This provides an incentive for market leaders to stay "on their toes", to be sure, but also to discount any long-term investment at a heavy risk premium, especially if it reduces the chances of immediate success. At this point, the reader may have spotted a seeming contradiction: if the physician "on top" keeps focusing on his short-term marketability and downplaying longer-term investments (such as his own retraining), isn't he implicitly digging his own grave in the long run? The answer is yes, of course, as this is precisely the nature of the dilemma.

This is what we could call "Hollywood economics", for it is how the Hollywood star system or the music industry work. The Hollywood

34

cinema industry is a very competitive industry with global reach. Every weekend, people in the whole world are free to choose what movie they want to watch, and they do so based on a few parameters such as the name of the featured actors or a trailer they saw last week. The cost of the theatre ticket for each one of them is minimal, but there is almost no limit to the number of people who can go to a given movie and, therefore, the potential revenue from a film can swing from zero (no one was interested) to many millions (everyone went to watch it, and some even went twice.). In other words: as in the case of the doctors after the barriers between the cities were removed, the difference between the physician (or, in this case, the actor) with the highest reputation and the one at the bottom of the ranking is potentially huge. The stakes are thus very high and the competition cut-throat. The salaries of the actors at the top of the ranking are an almost obscene multiple of those of many others who are only slightly less gifted, or have simply been a bit less lucky or a bit less ruthless.

So, the argument goes, our post-modern economy, increasingly global, competitive and meritocratic as it is, just cannot be excluded from this same rule. As competition grows, the pressure for here-and-now performance increases, which is of course a stimulating factor. Yet, at the same time, the planning horizon of corporations as well as individuals becomes shorter simply because no one can count on retaining his/her current position in the marketplace in the long run. The same way the salary levels of top stockbrokers and celebrity-CEO's are becoming strikingly similar to those of the most successful show business stars, so is the pressure on them to perform every single time, at every new round of the competitive game –only, the potential economic consequences of their mistakes are far more serious that a movie box office flop. By pushing their managers toward short decision time horizons and at the same time raising their personal stakes so high, companies would thus effectively be steering them towards gambles promising high short-term returns even if they jeopardise their firm's long-term prospects. From such gambles, of course, some companies would then emerge spectacularly successful, while others, like Enron or Barings, would end up in no less spectacular failures. Under this light, managerial myopia would appear as nothing more than an undesirable but probably unavoidable side effect of free market competition.

Yet the key question is still open: really, how damaging is this bias towards the short run? The answer is that it depends on the specific rules of the game. After all, what we are really saying is that the environment leads managers to evaluate investment opportunities by discounting their future expected cash flows at a higher rate. Under uncertainty, it is just rational and judicious to discount future investment outcomes at a higher rate than otherwise, precisely in order to attribute more weight in the decision to short-term cash in hand than to long-term, highly uncertain pie-in-the-sky prospects. One can easily think of many situations where a realistic focus on the here-and-now would actually be the right approach not only from the individual manager's viewpoint but also from that of the company as a whole. And, besides, the free market is an implacable judge, and has a particularly nasty way to punish those who focus too single-mindedly on the short run.

Take the physicians' case, for example. Even if the winner's rewards in every round are very high, if the game is going to be repeated under similar conditions many times afterwards we would be tempted to conclude that the short-term bias is not likely to be very damaging after all. Pitted against aggressive competitors who are willing to bet their all on the first round, a shrewd doctor might aim for an honourable second or third place at the start and then wait and see how his competitors' disregard for a long-term strategy eventually pulls them down to the bottom of the ranking. It is just as in a marathon: those who focus on being first in the first few hundreds of metres are often greeted with highly encouraging bursts of applause by the public, but rarely make it to the end of the race. Similarly, a free market has a way to punish those who fire all their bullets at the start of the battle. This is why it is only in amateur marathons that one can see runners starting the race as if it were a sprint only to fall down exhausted long before the end –in professional races, every runner tries to keep an optimal balance between speed and resistance, and therefore mid-race collapses are a rare event. Following the same logic, if all the runners in the marathon are professionals, it is among the ones racing ahead after the first few hundreds of metres that we should also expect to find the most likely winners. This is also why economic theory states, somewhat paradoxically, that, in a free, competitive market, it just makes sense to bet for the runners that prove to be the swiftest at the start of the race –i.e., to invest "myopically"[29]. Once again, Hollywood provides us with an excellent example: for all the rollercoaster uncertainty of show business, for all the aggressive short-term-ism movie producers are famous for, the fact is that most of the largest cinema studios of today can trace their roots straight back to the heroic days of silent movies[30].

Imagine now, however, that our ten physicians are not completely independent from each other –imagine, for example, that the winner of the first round gets to rule them all afterwards, and can impose on them a tax of some sort. Now the game has changed radically, because the winner can transfer the cost of his previous short-term focus to the other, less aggressive or less fortunate players. Then, what seemed like a cautious strategy of aiming at the beginning for second or third instead of first position in order to save for the long run becomes self-defeating, because those savings, as they are siphoned out by the ruler, will serve to make him all the more unbeatable in the long run. It is just as if, in our marathon example, the runner that completed the first round ahead of the others could then ask the others to carry him on their shoulders for the rest of the race. Under these conditions, we should indeed expect a strong short-term bias to take hold of the players' behaviour, even if the results are damaging for them all as a group. The physicians will focus on winning the first games and save very little for the long run. The marathon runners will race at full speed at the beginning even if this means damaging their performance for the rest of the competition. And, if the players are executives competing for the top job at their firm, they will also be willing to burn out the long-term viability of their departments for the sake of presenting better quarterly results.

*****

Let us assume now that, for whatever reason, we cannot avoid having one of the physicians placed in the position to rule and tax the others −for example, because they need to work together in a hospital, and someone has to act as the director. Is there still a way we could stimulate them to worry less about the short run? There is a way, although it may at first sound somewhat paradoxical. They could get together at the very beginning, throw dice and appoint the luckiest player as the ruler −in other words, they could take away the meritocratic, competitive component of the hierarchy. This way, the ruler would of course still represent the same burden, but at least there would be no need to embark in a costly internal tournament in the first rounds of the game. Notice that, in this new game, almost any arbitrary mechanism will work for the selection of the ruler *as long as it takes place before the start of the race*: family heritage, biological age, the result of tossing a coin −almost anything will do, *as long as it is independent from the players' actions*. To be sure, the lucky winner will not necessarily be the most capable for the role and, to the extent the group might have benefited from having a capable ruler, this will obviously constitute a disadvantage of this approach −but, if the personal advantages of becoming a ruler, and therefore the incentive of investing heavily in the initial tournament, are very high, the overall effect may still be positive.

This is the type of world Thomas Hobbes has in mind when, in 1652, he famously wrote that "during the time men live without a common power to keep them all in awe, they are in that condition which is called war; and such a war, as is of every man against every man." As a contemporary of the Thirty Years War and a direct witness of the English Civil Wars, he surely knew only too well what he was talking about. Nevertheless, if one key lesson should be drawn from this chapter is precisely that *there is no contradiction between the virtues of competition as Adam Smith described them and its evils according to Thomas Hobbes: what is different is the game each one of these authors implicitly assumed that was being played*. In

Smith's world, the contribution of each player can be clearly identified, and payment is easily enforced: the butcher, the brewer or the baker will only hand me their merchandise if I pay to them an agreed price in return[31]. As in the case of the physicians competing for the same patient pool, or in that of the marathon runners striving to be the first to cross the end line, their competition will act as a stimulus for each one to improve, and the result will be the highest average quality or the fastest race. Conversely, in Hobbes' world the common good depends on everyone's cooperation, but it is not possible to enforce adequate payment for each one's contribution and, therefore, an almighty ruling power (a *Leviathan*) is required to prevent people from shirking their duty. So, who was right? Strictly speaking, none of them was: in the real world there is always a combination of both elements at work. The more interdependent a process, the closer it will be to Hobbes' world —and vice versa, the less integrated, the closer to Smith's.

In sum: competition and integration do not mix well. Like milk and lemon, or like nitric acid and glycerine, they are fine things when in isolation but, together, can make a rather unpleasant combination. We started by asking ourselves whether, as the "Dilbert Principle" claims, the mechanisms of promotion to management positions may indeed have become even more inefficient than they used to be. Now we are starting to see the first components of an answer. Take our hierarchical physician community and assume the leader of the team is selected amongst the practicing doctors on the basis of length of tenure —itself quite a non-meritocratic promotion rule. Logically, leaders selected in this fashion could prove to be, in many cases, incompetent for this higher position —just as the "Peter Principle" would predict. But imagine, instead, that the promotion system becomes more competitive and it is now always the best physician, the one with the best reputation at the time of selection, who becomes the new leader. Then the capabilities of the promoted candidate may well be superior but, as we have seen, the physicians' behaviour will take a myopic bias whose negative consequences for the group may even be worse than the probability of selecting an incompetent was for the old system.

This is the root of the problem. In order to turn this insight into something we can use to analyse real business problems, however, we still need to dig a bit more into its basic rationale –as we will do in the next chapter.

# 4.    THE CORRUPTION OF POWER

> *"For the spirit of an organisation is created from the top. If an organisation is great in spirit, it is because the spirit of its top people is great. If it decays, it does so because the top rots; as the proverb has it: 'Trees die from the top'."*
>
> - Peter Drucker, *The Practice of Management*

I suspect the following scenario will ring an unpleasantly familiar bell for many professionals in a wide range of fields. A sales manager identifies a large potential opportunity at one of her clients –one that is too big for her to tackle alone, and will require the cooperation of other managers for the proposal to succeed. She highlights the opportunity, and a number of hands are quickly raised to volunteer help... in principle. Soon, however, it becomes evident that, while everyone wants to be *involved* in the proposal, no one is actually *committed* to it, as the other managers are assigning a higher priority to their own clients even when the opportunities they are targeting there are clearly inferior and, from the viewpoint of the firm as a whole, a lot less valuable. In the end, our frustrated manager can only cross her fingers and hope the other organisations that are competing for this specific opportunity will be just as short-sighted as her own.

This is only one of numerous possible examples of how the conflict between different individual interests within a corporation results in inefficient behaviour for the organisation as a whole. These conflicts are bound to happen whenever several people work together in a common process. Indeed, if people are free to choose, in a rational world they will only work together if the total product of their joint effort is worth the same or more than the sum of their individual outputs should they work separately. If the value of their joint effort is indeed higher than the sum of its parts, however, the question that immediately arises is how to split this difference between them, as it is never crystal-clear what contribution each one of the players has made to a shared enterprise. Every rational player will try to contribute as little as possible to the common effort, and grab as much as possible of the product of the group's activity. These common resources whose allocation is in dispute are thus, one could say, the real grapes of wrath.

Economists often represent this type of problem with a stylised scenario widely known as the "Prisoner's Dilemma". The story is just like the plot of an old cops' movie[32]. Two accomplices in crime (let's call them Albert and Bernard) are interrogated by the police in separate cells. They know that, if none of them confesses the crime, they will both be released because the police has no other evidence against them, whereas if they both accuse each other they will both be put in jail for, say, five years. But if Albert accuses Bernard and Bernard does not accuse him in turn (or vice versa, if Bernard accuses Albert but Albert remains silent), then the accuser will go free, whereas his accomplice will go to prison for, say, ten years both for the crime itself and for his lack of cooperation. Once isolated, then, *and if the game is only going to be played once*, the rational decision for Albert will be to betray Bernard because, regardless of whether Bernard has accused him or not, the outcome in either case is equal or better if he betrays him –either freedom or five years in jail, as opposed to either freedom or ten years. Exactly the same reasoning will apply to Bernard in respect to Albert. Hence, the rational decision for both of them is to betray each other, even though the outcome of this (which is for both to spend five years in prison) is to end up worse off than if they had not. Of course this is, at the core, the same problem our sales manager was facing: although the firm as a whole might benefit more from winning the big contract, the other managers get more credit from the sales they achieve at their own client accounts and, therefore, assign to them a higher priority.

One possible solution is repetition: if the game is played not once but many times, each prisoner has an incentive to cooperate with the other on the basis of the expectation that, otherwise, his accomplice will "take revenge" the next time and refuse to cooperate, thus pushing both into a worse scenario. Yet to the extent the outcome of the first rounds is more important than that of the last (say, if the player who is betrayed by his accomplice but does not betray in return is to be sent to the electric chair), or to the extent there is uncertainty about whether similar games are going to be played by the same players in the future, the effectiveness of this approach will be limited. The same applies to the sales manager in our first example. Other managers may decide to help her "altruistically" because they expect similar situations to arise in the future where they will be the ones needing help –but only to the extent their need to produce good results in the short run is not too overwhelming, and to the extent they expect to stay around long enough to eventually need help from the same colleagues in a not-too-distant future.

If repetition is not possible, or not enough to resolve the problem, an alternative solution can be applied: centralisation. This requires appointing a "general manager" to oversee compliance and punish those who do not cooperate. For a real organisation, this approach translates into the institution of a series of supervision and control roles with the power to impose punishments and rewards –in other words, a hierarchical system and a bureaucratic structure. For hierarchy and bureaucracy always go together: the purpose of bureaucratic controls is precisely to curtail the decision power of the players at the bottom of the chain of command and transfer it to the managers above them. Hence, hierarchy and bureaucracy, despite their evident shortcomings and the ease with which they degenerate into abuse, have a fundamental reason to exist in a social environment –and those who regard them as the root of all evil are thus a bit like the pigeon in Kant's parable, which, feeling the resistance of the air during flight, figured that it would be much easier to fly in the void.

The main problem with hierarchical structures is not so much that they represent a cost in themselves, or even that, by imposing controls, they tend to slow down production, but that they are run by human beings who are just as selfish as everyone else and who, precisely because their role is to supervise others, enjoy more autonomy and therefore have more opportunities to seek their personal advantage. It is as in the old saying: if the judge's role is to keep everyone else honest in town, whose role is it to keep the judge honest? The nature of any hierarchical structure is to create privileges, simply because those at the top have more freedom to shirk their duties, and thus pursue their own interest at the expense of the rest of the organisation. The more centralised an organisation, the higher the power its coordination roles will hold, and the more appealing the privileges of those in control will be. And the more attractive those privileges are, the more effort will other people be willing to divert to non-cooperative influence-seeking activities (in short, to office politics) in order to secure one of those positions for themselves.

We can therefore conclude that the organisation's non-cooperation costs will be higher when:

1.  The level of uncertainty in the future is high –i.e., the game is changing all the time and thus the incentives for an attitude along the lines of "I'll play fair with you now so that you play fair with me later" are lower.

2.  There is a more granular division of labour –i.e., the actions of the participants are more interdependent, each one of them is more specialised and therefore the production process relies more heavily on their cooperation.

We should already be familiar with this conclusion, for it is essentially the same we reached at the end of the previous chapter. Competition raises the level of uncertainty, and specialisation increases the dependency of the participants from each other. So, once again, we have to conclude that, while competition stimulates individual performance, and specialisation increases the process' productivity, these two elements do not mix well for, together, they all too often drive people to stab each other on the back.

*****

Sometimes it is useful to express ideas like these in graphical form: an image, they say, is worth more than a thousand words –even if it is an abstract image. In this case, we could represent the degree of integration (and therefore centralisation) as a vertical axis (and I know this requires the introduction of a number of technical assumptions that I will not make explicit here) and the level of competitive uncertainty as a horizontal one, as in Figure 1. Our disquisitions around the incompatibility of meritocracy and centralisation would then translate graphically into a "maximum productivity frontier" such that, for every level of uncertainty, there would be a degree of integration beyond which the overall costs of political backstabbing would exceed the benefits of the productivity gains from specialisation, and that this "optimal" degree of integration would be lower for a higher level of uncertainty.

We cannot know at this point what shape this frontier will take in the real world of course, as we have not specified the metrics we would use to measure either the degree of centralisation or that of uncertainty –yet we know its slope would be negative, that is, allowing for higher levels of centralisation the lower the level of competitive uncertainty.

**Figure 1**

*Integration
(specialisation,
centralisation)*

**EXCESS OF
POLITICS**

**LACK OF
COORDINATION**

*Frontier of
Maximum
Productivity*

0

*Uncertainty
(competition,
flexibility)*

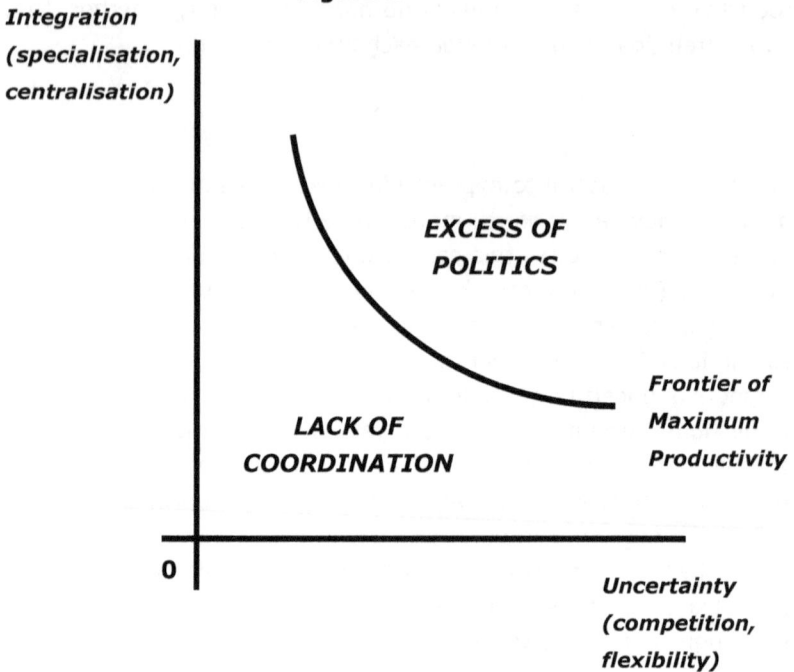

Evidently, every company will try to position itself somewhere on this frontier of maximum productivity; but to do so requires accepting some trade-offs:

A) The company can slide along the vertical axis by selecting a more or less "integrated" (i.e., centralised) production process. For example, a community of independent contractors who produce marketable goods separately from each other would score low on this axis, whereas a rigid production chain where every unit of finished product depends on the whole chain working smoothly would score high. The latter organisation presents, of course, the advantages of specialisation and economies of scale, but also requires tighter supervision and a centralised command –and therefore poses a starker Prisoner's Dilemma on its members.

B) Similarly, the company can also slide along the horizontal axis by selecting a more or less competitive promotion rule. Here, a company where all key positions were held by founding-family members would score low (i.e., to the left) on this axis, whereas one where the positions of command were assigned on the basis of a strictly meritocratic tournament would score high (i.e., to the right). Then again, the former approach would present the obvious disadvantages of selecting someone for a job regardless of his ability but, on the other hand, would be more effective at discouraging engagement in internal office politics.

Abstract as this may feel, there is quite a lot of empirical evidence that this inverse relationship between organisation uncertainty and centralisation exists. As early as in 1967, Paul Lawrence and Jay Lorsch, in their classical study *Organization and Environment*, found that the most successful businesses in fast-moving markets (e.g., specialty plastics) had significantly more decentralised organisations than their competitors, whereas top performers in comparatively stable, slow-moving markets (e.g., containers) were characterised by a higher level of centralisation than their rivals[33]. Similarly, firms whose key leadership roles are occupied by founding-family members (and whose structure is therefore less meritocratic than in otherwise comparable corporations) also tend to present more centralised structures than their competitors. Government-controlled companies are usually much more bureaucratic in their internal dynamics than their private competitors of similar size, even if the reasons for their nationalisation had in principle nothing to do with the government's interventionist agenda (think, for example, of Renault in France). Businesses operating in heavily-regulated markets tend to be more bureaucratic than otherwise –think, for instance, of retail banking, insurance or utilities... In short, the evidence generally confirms our intuition: centralisation requires internal cooperation, and cooperation is the antithesis of competition.

*****

EDUARD GRACIA

The manager's role in an organisation is to ensure cooperation takes place. This is the underlying meaning of that oft-repeated (and abused) statement, "leadership is about trust" –or, more generally, of Peter Drucker's famous dictum, "the one requirement for a manager is integrity"[34]. The role of the manager is to make sure the conflicts we illustrated with the Prisoner's Dilemma are, if not eliminated, at least reduced to a minimum within the framework of the enterprise; but, for this to work, the manager needs to credibly offer to cooperate in return. Thus, in the "excess of politics" section of Figure 1, the problem is that lack of cooperation among the players is so damaging (or, alternatively, the bureaucratic controls required to ensure they keep cooperating are so paralyzing) that the combined advantages of synergies and meritocracy are overturned – and managers, as the players with the widest freedom of action, are those in whom this type of behavior becomes most evident. In other words: *when an organisation suffers from widespread lack of cooperation, its management is likely to be the sickest of all.*

Here is thus the crux of the problem: those who have the power to steer an organisation away from trouble are very often those who have the most vested interest in the preservation of the *status quo*. Therefore, when an organisation finds itself in the "excess of politics" area in Figure 1, there is tension between forces pulling in different directions, and the result is not always positive. On the one hand, although the leadership of an organisation can, to a certain extent, adjust its degree of internal competition by redesigning pay and promotion mechanisms appropriately, in the long run the organisation's ability to "buffer away" external competitive pressure is limited. For instance, even if a company does not explicitly transmit the risk generated by external conditions directly onto its employees, the pressure of the financial markets' penalisation under the form of an abnormally high cost of capital and/or the loss of the best and brightest employees to better paid or more promising jobs with the competition will eventually force it to internalise the competitive pressure from outside. On the other hand, moving down along the vertical axis of integration represents the elimination of hierarchical privileges, and thus will tend to be opposed by those who benefit from them. Indeed, as Michael Jensen[35] points out, empirical evidence indicates that, particularly in large organisations that have enjoyed commanding market positions for long periods of time, "the culture of the organization and the mindset of managers seem to make it extremely difficult for [downwards] adjustment to take place until long after the problems have become severe, and in some cases even unsolvable."

This is why they say that "fish stink from the head" –or, as Peter Drucker put it, somewhat more elegantly, "trees die from the top." Bureaucratic hierarchies are purposefully designed to detract decision power from the bottom and concentrate it at the top. Therefore, the freedom of action to engage in self-serving political activities exists at the top much more abundantly than at the bottom, and will be much more so the more centralised the hierarchy is. The power to heal a team is thus frequently in the same hands that are keeping it sick in the first place. This is why organisations under pressure so often display the bizarre spectacle of leaders trying every possible remedy except the one that would obviously resolve the problem or, even worse, sitting tight and feigning serenity while the ship sinks under their feet.

# 5.   ORGANISATIONS UNDER STRESS

*"Nearly all men can stand adversity; but if you want to test a man's character, give him power."*

- Abraham Lincoln

Sam Spade, the main character in Dashiell Hammett's novel *The Maltese Falcon*, held that the best way to understand how a mechanism works is to stick an iron bar in-between the cogs and then see where it breaks. Despite the *pulp* brutality of the image, he actually had a good point: the easiest way to spot the political links within a human organisation is to put it under stress until it reaches breaking point –only we, fortunately, instead of having to stick the iron bar ourselves, can look back into the past to find examples of organisations where such a crisis already took place.

We are not interested in just any type of crisis, of course: what we want to see now is what happens when, for whatever reason, an organisation that was positioned more or less on the "maximum productivity frontier" is pushed into the "excess of politics" sector of the graph. This, as we have seen, can take place either because the level of uncertainty for the team members has increased while the organisation structure remained the same (a move like A→B in Figure 2) or because the structure has become more centralised without reducing the level of meritocratic pressure on the players (a shift like A→C in Figure 2):

**Figure 2**

*Integration (specialisation, centralisation)*

**EXCESS OF POLITICS**

C

A    B

*Frontier of Maximum Productivity*

**LACK OF COORDINATION**

0

*Uncertainty (competition, flexibility)*

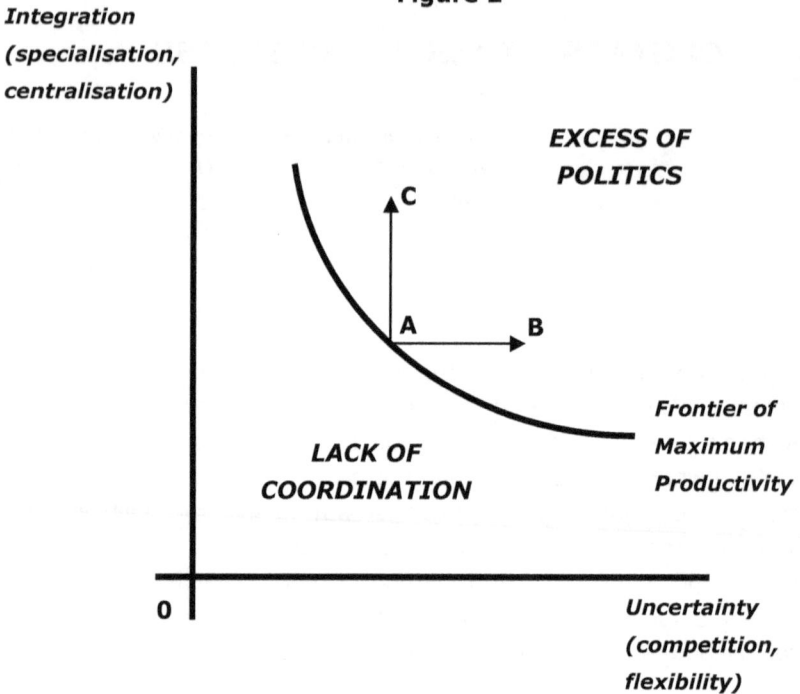

It is not difficult to find examples of either type. Among the recent instances of A→B moves, maybe one of the most clear-cut is that of Marks & Spencer. Indeed, the case of M&S is particularly interesting not only because it is so recent and well known, but also, crucially, because it is relatively easy to trace back exactly when the shift started. It will therefore also help us highlight a very important trait of the "excess of politics" area: although the issues may soon become evident to insiders, their real impact can take a very long time to surface on the accounting bottom line.

Since its foundation in 1894, M&S had been an old-style, paternalistic, strongly hierarchical business where the role of the chairman was always played by a member of the founding family[36]. Throughout the long tenure of the founder's son, Lord Simon Marks (chairman from 1916 to 1964), M&S had grown to become Britain's number one retailer. The firm offered to most of its employees a job for life at an organisation where promotion took place primarily within the ranks. Decisions were highly centralised, and positions of command were rewarded with privileges that were the envy of the competition –such as executive dining rooms, flight rights on the company jet and the like. In the course of many decades, the company grew steadily to become the most emblematic brand in British retail business. Then, in 1984, Lord Marcus Sieff, the last founding-family chairman, retired and left the top job to a man that deserved it on merits alone: Derek Rayner, a capable executive who had risen from the ranks and who, on moving to his new role, explicitly made a commitment to try to keep things, as much as possible, the way they had always been.

Yet, despite the best intentions, the appointment of a non-family member was bound to upset the delicate web of incentives and expectations of those who worked at the firm. Suddenly, the perspective of promotion to the chairman role was more of a reality for every one of the top executives around Lord Rayner. Thus, in her analysis of this period, Judi Bevan quotes one of the founding-family members according to whom "we felt things did begin to change under Derek. He kept the values but managers became more competitive and status conscious with each other." The pressure inevitably spread like fire all the way down the hierarchy: as a then-junior M&S executive explained to Bevan, "Derek started to squeeze the business for profit and the organisation became more political. You always had to mind your back." This is, of course, exactly what one would expect to see in an organisation moving from A to B as depicted in Figure 2. The company was just as hierarchical and centralised as it had always been, no more –but now the incentives for each one of the executives to try to outperform the others in the short run were higher.

Gradually, the problem became worse. Under the leadership of Sir Richard Greenbury, who succeeded Rayner at the helm in 1991, the profitability of the business steadily grew up to reach an astonishing profit-on-sales ratio of over 14% sustained throughout 1997 and 1998 –the highest on record since the company's flotation in 1927, and the highest of any large retailer at the time except Wal-Mart. Alas, the feat was achieved to a large extent through cost control measures that, with hindsight, are easy to link to the causes that would eventually bring about the downfall. Staff costs were significantly reduced: for example, the average retail space served per employee increased by a staggering 25% in seven years –from 165 square feet in 1991 to 205 in 1998. And staff numbers were not the only cost reduction item: training expenses were severely reduced, and even budgets for running trials of new clothing lines (which in the retail business constitute a usual way to reduce the risk of a new launch) were cut down. Bevan even quotes a store manager "who recalled his horror on being ordered to put the price up on a line of dresses that had gone particularly well", for, as he explained, "in the old days, if a line went well, you moved heaven and earth with your suppliers to get more –you never, ever put the price up." In April 1998, the director of strategic planning issued a report where, not surprisingly, he pointed out that the customer base was growing increasingly dissatisfied –but, at the time, profits were still at record levels, so the report ended up having a rather minimal impact... Yet perhaps it was already too late to avoid the blow anyway: on 3 November 1998, M&S had to announce a 23% fall in the company's half-year profit ending in September –the most serious profit setback since the Second World War. By the end of the fiscal year, in mid-1999, profits had fallen still further down to a mere 54% of the previous year's peak.

How could this possibly happen? And, most intriguingly, how could the crisis take the management team so utterly by surprise? Bevan's meticulous account describes how, from 1993 onwards, political pressures steadily mounted up as Greenbury (a capable and energetic but also fairly autocratic leader) refused to provide any clear signal towards the designation of a successor and, instead, lobbied to extend his tenure beyond his originally scheduled retirement date in 1996, when he would turn 60. Furthermore, he was effectively the last member of the "old guard" of M&S executives whose early career had developed under the legendary shadow of Simon Marks. While this "gilded generation" had been in power, succession had been tacitly expected to take place within its ranks – but now that Greenbury himself, who had long been the *enfant terrible* of the group, was reaching retirement age himself, the game was up. His successor could potentially be any of the executives of the next generation group... Only, he did not seem ready to single out any one of them as his *dauphin* just yet.

In the absence of any clear alternative candidate for the role within the executive team, and keeping in mind the excellent business results Greenbury had been able to deliver so far, the board decided to postpone his retirement. Nevertheless, in the minutes of the board's meeting, dated 2 August 1995, it was explicitly stated that the extension was only valid until Greenbury would reach the age of 62, and that "any period of office thereafter [would] be reviewed by the board on an annual basis". By 1998, however, Greenbury had not designated any clear successor yet, was again seeking support for another extension and thus, not surprisingly, was driving uncertainty amid the ambitious executive team to white-hot levels. The organisation was, as a result, sliding ever deeper into the "excess of politics" sector in our Figure 2.

When an organisation faces a severe crisis, things tend to get worse before they get better –and M&S was unfortunately no exception to the rule. Crises always increase uncertainty, and this in turn intensifies even more the political struggles within the firm. In 1999, prompted by the poor business results, one of the executives even headed what can only be described as a plot (which, by the way, misfired) to take over the chairman's role. There would be no point, however, in reviewing here all the twists and turns of the sad story of those years –suffice it to say that the deep dive continued and, by mid-2001, profits hit a record low at about 40% of their April 1998 peak. Turning the fortunes of the company around took not only a brand new leadership team, but also a radical restructuring of the organisation. The new team, under chairman Luc Vandevelde, proceeded to decentralise M&S, which required not only to become "leaner at the top" (i.e., to fire scores of entrenched middle-to-high-level managers) but also, as Bevan puts it, to transform the firm "from a despotic, bureaucratic, paternalistic institution to a modern, responsive corporation where every staff member was accountable and encouraged to be entrepreneurial." In terms of our Figure 2, thus, the organisation had to slide down from point B to meet the frontier of maximum productivity below.

I must insist once again, though: there are no villains in this story. Like Alice in Wonderland, or like the characters in Kafka's tales, each individual tried to behave rationally in a seemingly irrational world – yet it was the very rationality of their individual decisions that, like in the Prisoner's Dilemma, led them straight to disaster. And, like in a Greek tragedy, all the ominous signs were there for a long while, but none of the main characters was able to see them... For the gods always blind first those whose pride they intend to punish.

*****

Instances of companies sliding upwards along the A→C arrow are just as frequent. One typical instance sometimes arises when companies deploy new Enterprise Integration software systems (also known, somewhat inappropriately, as Enterprise Resource Planning or "ERP" systems), such as SAP, Oracle or PeopleSoft. In the more integrated, interconnected environment that results from these implementations, many decisions that used to have only a local impact start to have enterprise-wide ramifications which justify a certain increase in the level of centralisation. Yet systems integration is frequently used in enterprises, for political ends, as an excuse to centralise strategic functions beyond what the software and the process rationalisation really require. The resulting IT shared services departments thus often behave with the inefficiency and disregard for quality and client satisfaction that characterise monopolies.

An example from my own personal experience may help to illustrate this point. A large European bank decided to replace its complex landscape of accounting, consolidation and group reporting systems with an ERP software solution. The idea was to hold the General Ledgers and related functions of all its subsidiaries in a central system from which the group consolidation and reporting systems would be populated. In the past, the general ledgers, the group consolidation and reporting systems, and the Excel sheets that were used as the main planning device had not been integrated technologically and, as a result, required a lot of manual work, including manual data transfers and reconciliation exercises. Nonetheless, the overall process worked because the support teams were typically local (often physically close to the end users), knowledgeable (many had also "fathered" the systems they were maintaining), and non-bureaucratic. Since one of the key advantages of the new technology solution was its integration, it made sense to create a large "centre of expertise" to support it, with the expectation that the resulting synergies would reduce the overall cost of support. Yet things did not go exactly as planned. Because the support centre was so large, its leadership became a power centre in itself. Soon, there was a political push to centralise support functions that would have been more effective had they remained close to the end users, whatever the underlying software.

In addition, the centre's leadership aggressively pursued cost reduction, which was one of the most visible drivers of change and one of the most politically rewarded performance factors. To do this, management hired very unqualified –and therefore relatively inexpensive– personnel. Unable to depend upon these resources to perform their jobs efficiently, the centre's leadership instead relied on a heavy bureaucratic structure to keep the system moving. This approach was applied to other cost items, such as machine sizing, for the same reasons: the hardware costs were highly visible, whereas the costs of poor system performance at end-user level were not.

The two prongs of this strategy, cost reduction and bureaucracy, supported each other, at least for a while. Perhaps fortunately, the leaders of the support centre were too aggressive in their pursuit of short-term cost reductions at the expense of long-term performance for, eventually, end-user complaints became so loud that they reached the highest levels of the organisation. This led to an external audit of the "centre of expertise", after which its leader was invited to leave, scarcely three years after the new system had been put in place.

*****

It is not only the introduction of new technology, though, that can trigger this type of crisis. In this sense, the case of the Ford Motor Co. in the first half of the 20th Century constitutes an extreme example of how pursuing a highly integrated (i.e., centralised) production model can first be a source of competitive advantage and then, if pushed beyond certain limits, become a serious handicap. Of all the captains of industry of his generation, Henry Ford was no doubt the one that pressed furthest in this direction, and the company he founded was the first to apply the chain production principles systematically to as complex a product as an automobile. It was this that enabled the Ford Motor Co. to mass-produce the famous *Model T* at a unit cost far below that of any of its competitors. By the spring of 1914, with its moving assembly line operating steadily, Ford's Highland Park factory in Detroit had managed to reduce the average labour time per car from 12 hours and 8 minutes to a mere 1 hour and 33 minutes[37] –a record achievement even by our 21st Century standards. In the 1920s, Ford's new plant at River Rouge, at the time the largest factory in the world, would achieve even higher levels of efficiency.

Yet the price of such an efficient process was integration, and the price of integration was vulnerability: in a production chain, if a single workplace along the chain stops, the whole chain stops. Hence, Ford's plants became famous for their meticulous attention to detail and the clockwork precision of their production chains –which, in turn, was made possible by the almost military discipline that was imposed on the workers. Rouge had the reputation of being the most immaculately clean and meticulously planned production plant in the world −even drinking water temperature was there subject to precise regulation[38]. To be sure, there was a price to pay to ensure the workers' willingness to accept such levels of discipline in a production process that, after all, would have been all too easy for strikers to disrupt: Henry Ford paid the highest salaries in the country. This is most likely what he meant when he described his 1914 wage raise to $5 for an 8-hour day (at a time when the average U.S. industrial worker made about $11 a week) as "one of the finest cost-cutting moves we ever made"[39]: salaries well above market level were the price he had to pay for a docile workforce. He did not stop there: in 1918 Ford's shop floor wages were raised again to an unheard-of $6 per day, and in 1926 the company introduced the five-day, forty-hour work week.

All this made perfect business sense. As so often happens with autocrats, however, Henry Ford's personality was to push the degree of centralisation of his business far beyond the boundaries of not just business but plain common sense. After 1919, when he bought out his partners, the Dodge brothers, and thus became the sole owner of the firm, he started to systematically fire anyone who would dare to make any decisions instead of limiting himself to following his orders slavishly. This, of course, included his most competent managers − which probably felt like a godsend to his competitors: almost immediately after being dismissed by Ford, both his production chief, William Knudsen, and his sales head, Norval Hawkins, took over the same posts at General Motors[40]. During the 1920s, and even more the 1930s, the command-and-control approach at Ford was brought to such an extreme that the company almost literally did away with its middle management, in the sense that, while of course a number of people would perform the routine planning and supervision task, all the decision-making power was concentrated at the very top. Peter Drucker[41] aptly compared the system to a sort of Soviet Russia where Mr. Ford would play the role of Stalin whilst the infamous Harry Bennett, a former Navy boxer whose only managerial credentials were his well-known reputation for brutality and his connections to the Detroit underworld, played that of the secret police chief. In terms of our Figure 2, therefore, Ford was undergoing a shift along the lines of the A→C arrow.

The Ford Motor Company did indeed turn into a dark place of political intrigue whose history reads very much like that of a totalitarian regime. Harry Bennett became Henry Ford's right hand, the shadow behind the throne, effectively overruling the company's president, Henry Ford's son Edsel –who would die in 1943 as a result of a stomach cancer that most attributed to the accumulated tension of dealing for years with both Bennett's pressure and his own father's antics. The thugs in Bennett's "Service Department" played the role of an internal Gestapo, spying on everyone from executives to shop floor workers. Suspected trade union sympathisers were often hauled off and beaten up senseless before being fired on trumped-up charges of starting a fight. Benjamin Stolberg, the famous trade union leader, described the situation at Rouge in 1938 as follows:

> "There are about 800 underworld characters in the Ford Service organization. They are the Storm Troops. They make no pretence of working, but are merely 'keeping order' in the plant community through terror. Around this nucleus are, however, between 8,000 and 9,000 authentic workers, a great many of them spies and stool pigeons. Because of this highly organized terror and spy system, the fear in the plant is something indescribable." [42]

Unchecked power turned short, stocky Bennett into such a farcical villain character that one would doubt of the reality of his exploits if they were not so well documented. He always carried one or two pistols with him, and occasionally used them to assert his authority at the Rouge plant: once he shot a cigar out of a man's mouth, another time it was a man's hat –while he held it. He even kept several pet lions in his mansion-castle on Geddes Road in Ann Arbor, and would occasionally bring one of them with him to the Rouge works.

The surveillance conditions over the members of the management team were certainly less brutal, but only marginally less onerous. Over time, therefore, those among Ford's most capable managers who had not already been fired fled for better opportunities elsewhere. The results were felt under the form of gradual profit and market share erosion, mild at first but progressively more painful as the company kept losing ground. According to Alfred Chandler's authoritative study[43], in 1921 Ford accounted for 55.7% of all the passenger cars in the USA, whereas General Motors represented only a 12.3%. By 1929, before the Great Depression struck, Ford's market share had already fallen down to a 31.3%, for the first time behind that of General Motors with 32.3%, and followed by the fast growing 8.2% of a new challenger, the Chrysler Corporation. Even worse was to come. By 1940, Ford's share of the passenger vehicles market had faded to a mere 18.9%, far behind not only General Motors' 47.5% but also Chrysler's 23.7%. The company was but a shadow of its former self. Concern about its decline reached such levels during World War II that the Roosevelt administration seriously considered lending Studebaker (the fourth of Detroit's car makers, but much smaller than any of the Big Three) the money to buy out Ford or even, as an alternative, to nationalise the firm altogether in order to ensure war supplies.

In short, unlike Soviet Russia, the Ford Motor Co. simply could not isolate itself from the surrounding economic environment, and paid the price for trying to do so under the form of profitability and market share. Hence, when Henry Ford II, after succeeding his namesake grandfather at the helm of the company on 21 September 1945 (and after firing Bennett barely a few minutes thereafter), started to hire a new layer of professional managers and to move towards a more flexible, management-by-objectives leadership style, all he was really doing was to realign Ford's internal structures to the realities of its environment.

The Ford case is particularly revealing because it highlights another simple but often forgotten truth: no company exists in isolation. Although in the short and medium run a firm's leadership can often define the internal conditions of competitive pressure among its members independently from the environment, in the long run no company can afford to ignore the market imperative forever. Sometimes, as we have seen, the impact takes a long while to make itself felt throughout the firm, and even longer to trigger a reaction: about fifteen years in the case of Marks & Spencer, even longer in that of the Ford Motor Company. Yet, in the long run, not even Henry Ford could steer his ship forever against the tide.

This logically raises another question: what happens if, instead of the company's internal structure, it is the environment that changes unexpectedly over time? Imagine, for example, that the level of uncertainty and competitive pressure increased for a given market sector, or for the overall economy. Sooner or later, the internal organisation of corporations would need to adapt, or else pay the price of staying above the maximum productivity frontier –but, as we have also seen, when a company moves into the "excess of politics" space there are many internal pressures to avoid the necessary adjustment. This is why there can be such a long lag between the beginning of a problem and the adoption of a solution – and, in many cases, a major crisis needs to blow up before the wheels start to move in the right direction. The only difference is of course that, if it were the whole economic environment of a sector or a country what changed, instead of the conditions specific to a particular corporation, then obviously *most* (if not *all*) the businesses would find themselves going through a similar crisis at the same time.

We have already seen how, for the last thirty years or so, the economic environment has indeed turned faster, riskier and more intensely competitive. Even before we take a closer look at the historical facts, should we not expect this to throw most large corporations into the "excess of politics" space in Figure 2? We logically should –and, as we will see throughout the next two chapters, there is abundant evidence suggesting that this is indeed what has actually happened.

# 6.  THE PENDULUM OF HISTORY

*"Few discoveries are more irritating than those which expose the pedigree of ideas."*

- Lord Acton, *The History of Freedom and Other Essays*

Arguably, modern management thought was born, in the halcyon days of Frederick Taylor and Henry Ford, as a "scientific" framework to achieve efficiency gains through systematic division of labour. Not that this was by any means a novel idea, as much as Taylor and Ford may have wanted to make it look so. After all, Adam Smith's use of a pin factory to illustrate the advantages of division of labour in his *Wealth of Nations* bears witness of the widespread application of this technique in 18th Century Britain: "one man draws out the wire, another straights it, a third cuts it, a fourth points it, a fifth grinds it at the top for receiving the head"... No even then was this a new concept: it was but a production chain *avant la lettre* that enabled the specialised workers of the Venetian Arsenal in the Renaissance to turn out fully-equipped warships in a matter of hours when operating at peak[44]. So when, around 1900, Taylor's theories started to take hold, the fundamental principle underlying them was old news indeed. Industrial-scale production was not a novelty either: in Great Britain, the Industrial Revolution was already over a hundred years old. Although the USA, like most countries in Continental Europe, drastically improved its transportation network with the wave of railway development that took place around 1870, by that time the networks of England and Belgium had already been quite well developed for over twenty years, and water transportation had been using canals, steamers and copper-bottomed clippers for even longer. Yet it was not in Britain, the undisputed factory of the world for most of the 19th Century, but in the U.S. and in several countries of Continental Europe where the new "scientific" management techniques were first adopted towards the end of the century. Why? And why did this happen precisely then?

The history of international commerce throughout most of the 19th Century can be represented, at a very high level, as a slow but steady march towards free trade. It was a globalisation era not unlike our own, where Great Britain played a role somewhat similar to the one the United States plays today. Around 1870, however, a number of countries started a gradual process of increasing tariff barriers to protect their local industries against foreign competition. It is significant, from this viewpoint, that the Civil War has traditionally been regarded as the starting point of the American mass-production era that eventually led to the first applications of Taylor's theories, for it was precisely with the war, and specifically with the Morrill Act of 1861, that the protectionist era began. Starting from a very low point in 1860, by 1864 the average tariff rate in the USA had already gone up to 47%. In Continental Europe, the shift to protectionism began a bit later, but quickly took hold nearly everywhere as a consequence of the Great Depression of 1873-1879, as the industrial interests in every country lobbied to ask their governments for protection from external competitors. By the end of the 19th Century, only Great Britain, Denmark and the Netherlands remained loyal to the principles of free trade[45].

So the economies of countries like Germany, France or the USA protected themselves against foreign competition –i.e., they reduced the level of competition they were exposed to, thus following the direction we have indicated on Figure 3 with the solid arrow A→B. As a result, they gave up some of the benefits of free trade, such as the ability to buy supplies from wherever the best quality/price relationship could be found. Yet this new, "tamer" business environment also opened a new set of previously untapped opportunities to take advantage of a finer division of labour –in other words, companies in the United States or in Germany could improve their productivity by moving along the dotted line from B to C in Figure 3. The business world was now ready for the benefits of rigid, meticulously planned production chains, and needed people who could devise how the new concept would work. This was the role the first paladins of "scientific management", like Frederick Taylor in the U.S. or Henri Fayol in France, were to play.

**Figure 3**

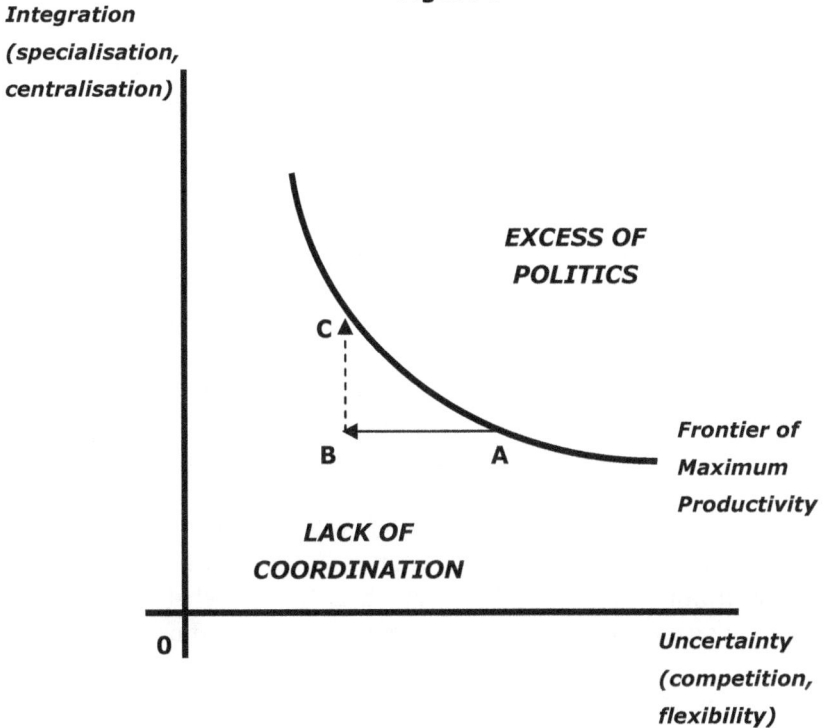

Thus, the new protected environments played the role of greenhouses for most of our modern industrial empires. The years between the American Civil War (or, in Europe, the unification of Germany and Italy) and the First World War saw the birth of corporate titans like Standard Oil, U.S. Steel, Ford, General Motors, General Electric, Westinghouse, Bell (later to become AT&T) or IBM in America, or like AEG, Bayer, BASF, Hoechst or Daimler-Benz in Germany.

We would search in vain for comparably wide-ranging industrial mammoths in the century of industrialisation before 1860. It was not that previous generations lacked their fair share of daring, successful entrepreneurs. Men like Richard Arkwright, who in 1771 built and operated in England the first textile factory powered by a watermill, often accumulated considerable fortunes, but did not found time-defying business empires. Other successful entrepreneurs of the same generation, like Robert Peel, Robert Owen or the Crawshay family, followed very similar paths. Not even the famous Boulton & Watt Co., the Birmingham-based engineering firm that held the patent of James Watt's revolutionary steam engine for a quarter of a century (until 1800), was ever able to successfully diversify beyond its core skills and, as steam technology was gradually replaced throughout the second half of the 19th Century, slowly faded away. The next generation of engineers-cum-entrepreneurs was not different in this respect. For all the fame (and money) that early-to-mid 19th Century engineers like Robert Fulton, George Stephenson or Isambard Kingdom Brunel deservedly gained, they did not leave behind leading corporations like those that Henry Ford or Alexander Graham Bell were to found by the end of the century. The same could be said of the men that amassed the largest fortunes of the day, as Cornelius Vanderbilt did with steamship and railroad transportation, or John Jacob Astor with real estate speculation in a fast-growing New York City: they left behind long-lasting patrimonies, but not long-lasting business organisations.

Even those few among the modern giants that, like DuPont, can trace their roots to before 1870 actually remained relatively small until after this date. Indeed, the firm that Eleuthère Irénée du Pont de Nemours, a French chemist and intellectual escaping from the terrors of revolutionary France, founded in Pennsylvania in 1802, did not extend its product range beyond its original core skills (the manufacturing of black gunpowder) until 1880, and only after this date started to grow from a medium-sized firm into the diversified chemicals giant DuPont is today[46]. A similar story can be told about the famous Krupp steel mills in Germany. Although the family name appears in the merchants' guild register of the city of Essen since

1587, and is known to have owned an iron forge at least since 1800, the business remained relatively small until the 1870s. Still in 1845, the Krupp steel mill in Essen did not employ more than a hundred people; at the time of Alfred Krupp's death in 1887, it already employed 45,000, plus another 30,000 employed at other works outside Essen.

This was not due to any self-limiting blindness on the part of the early entrepreneurs, but to the implacable logic of a highly competitive market governed by free trade. In this environment, lack of focus is lethal, for a company can only succeed by striving to be the best in a particular niche market. Thus, for instance, Boulton & Watt became the go-to workshop to buy highly-reliable steam engines at least until the 1830s, and DuPont was the U.S. Government's primary gunpowder supplier for most of the 19th Century. In other words, these firms grew by doing more of the same, while avoiding, to the extent possible, the risk of extending into uncharted territory.

At a different scale, it was a bit as in the modern Information Technology sector –a high dynamism business if there ever was one. As the IT market matures, it tends to self-organise into well-defined niches dominated by one or two major players: Intel for microprocessors, Microsoft for PC applications, Oracle (followed by Microsoft) for large databases, SAP (followed by Oracle) for enterprise applications... Scale acts as a powerful ally for the company that dominates a specific niche when it comes to competing against a smaller newcomer. In recent years we have seen many instances where one of these smaller players has been cornered, absorbed or simply wiped out by a larger rival: Lotus, Netscape, Informix, Baan, PeopleSoft, etc. Yet, despite the obvious theoretical advantages of economies of scope (starting with the privileged access to a semi-captive clientele the larger firms enjoy), it is extremely difficult for the leader of a particular niche to extend successfully into another, whatever its scale. Examples abound: the unsuccessful attempts by IBM and later Microsoft to penetrate the enterprise applications market, the expensive failure of Hewlett-

Packard's aggressive expansion programme under Carly Fiorina's leadership, Intel's near-monopoly of the microprocessors market (recently highlighted by Apple's decision to buy its microprocessors from Intel instead of IBM going forward)... In short: when a market is subject to so much competitive uncertainty that it approximates a winner-take-all game, scale is often not so much the cause as the consequence of success, and scope, to the extent it leads to lack of focus, can even turn into a false friend.

Thus, when a man who had made a fortune with industrial activities in the early days of the Industrial Revolution, like Arkwright or Peel, wanted to diversify his risk, the right approach was not to extend the business into adjacent markets where it held no particular comparative advantage, but rather to reinvest part of his wealth in unrelated assets: land, debt, shares of other businesses, etc. It was therefore not these industrial enterprises but the banks that financed them, and therefore found a business advantage in hedging their financial bets through scale and diversification, that founded most of the large business organisations that have lasted from the First Industrial Revolution to our days. In fact, nearly all of today's largest U.K. retail banks (Barclays, Lloyds TSB, Royal Bank of Scotland...) can trace the roots back to even before 1770 –the most notable exception being HSBC, which "only" goes back to 1865.

This goes a long way toward explaining why British industrial enterprises, unlike their German or American rivals, remained comparatively small after 1880, displayed such reluctance to make the large investments required for modern mass production and preferred to organise themselves as small firms coordinated through flexible institutions such as the textile federations. For British industry lived in the more uncertain world outside the tariff-protected incubators of America or Continental Europe and, thus, its investment horizons were logically more short-term-focused.

*****

Some might argue that this interpretation of events flies on the face of conventional wisdom. Many accounts of the period after 1870 (aptly known as the Second Industrial Revolution), particularly those centred on the sequence of events in the United States, tend to emphasise the unprecedented volumes of demand and the opportunities for economies of scale they opened. But this does not explain why the change took so long to take hold in Great Britain. After all, Britain was, by the mid-19th Century, the first (and only) mass consumer society, and its position at the apex of the industrial ranking was afterwards only slowly eroded by the newcomers. The volumes of British steel production remained higher than those of either the USA or Germany until around 1895, and the British textile industry was still the largest generator of demand for synthetic dyes by the turn of the century [47]. Other, more "cultural" or "psychological" explanations have also been put forward: it has been argued, for example, that the problem resided in the more conservative nature of the British society. Yet, while this explanation might just work in a comparison with the USA, it is hard to defend that Imperial Germany, where members of the Prussian petty nobility (the "*Junker*") occupied most if not all the key positions in the Government and the Army, was any less conservative a society than Britain.

Similarly, it has also been said that the reluctance of British universities to focus their teaching on "practical" subjects such as engineering, as opposed to just being a place to develop gentlemen, represented a crucial difference. But, again, it is difficult to see how those German universities where aristocratic students displayed proudly their duelling scars in drinking parties, and where Jewish students with scientific interests specialised in pure mathematics because access to laboratories was so routinely denied to them, would have turned into developers of an engineering class had they not been under a market pressure that the British industry simply did not exert. Indeed, the comparison between Britain, Germany and the USA is extremely useful here because it allows us to exclude most of the hypothesis that might just seem to work in a more restricted analysis. There is absolutely no relevant geographic, economic or cultural feature that would make Imperial Germany look similar to the United States and at the same time different from the British Empire in the late 19th Century except for its protectionist policy. If only by exclusion, one is thus compelled to admit that this must be the reason for the divergent reactions of these countries to the Second Industrial Revolution.

How did a tightly integrated production chain also lead to large, vertically-integrated industrial empires in these countries? Mr. Richardson told us the answer loud and clear in Chapter 2. Remember? We read there how this executive indoctrinated the trainees of the Vicks School of Applied Merchandising never to hesitate to sacrifice a loyal supplier if an alternative vendor was able to offer slightly better conditions. Of course, if these are the rules of the game, what vendor in his right mind would be willing to specialise to produce supplies exactly to Vicks' specifications, as opposed to sticking to a more generic product range? Yet a smooth production chain requires inputs to be produced exactly to specification... The solution to the dilemma was obvious: if Vicks or any other firm needed a perfectly dedicated supplier, it would need to own it. This is also why Henry Ford, the first and foremost advocate of integrated production processes, was also the one that brought the principles of vertical integration to their most extreme expression, buying steel mills, mines and even rubber plantations to produce the inputs for his automobiles. In his last years, Ford was no doubt bringing these principles way too far, and was damaging his firm by doing so –but there was still a method in his madness.[48]

At a macroeconomic level, it is true, globalisation continued to expand at least until the First World War –in fact, a number of authors go so far as to describe the period between 1870 and 1914 as "the first globalisation wave" [49] , comparable only to the subsequent one that started after World War II. It was in this period, for instance, when most industrialised nations (France, Germany, the USA...) followed the lead of the British Empire in adopting the Gold Standard, which effectively amounted to a monetary union where gold acted as the single global currency. Yet, although international trade was still growing, tariff rearmament started to take its toll. Recent estimates indicate that the total value of world trade as a percentage of global Gross Domestic Product (GDP) [50] grew, on average, at a 3% compound annual rate between the end of the Napoleonic Wars in 1815 and the start of the new protectionist wave in 1870, but only at a 1.7% a year between 1870 and 1914.

Then, in 1914, as if tariff protection were not enough, the Great War burst. Global trade was disrupted. The International Gold Standard was suspended at all the countries that participated in the war. The war also prompted large-scale, government-financed demand for industrial products. Bids for Army (or, for that matter, public-sector) supply contracts are famously bureaucratic and, to the extent the volumes involved are necessarily large, usually restricted to the few bidders that can demonstrate the production capacity required to fulfil them. Thus, the stress was placed even more heavily on economies of scale, and hence also on meticulous production planning. The interaction between the war effort and the first stages of modern management thought should not be underestimated: for instance, James McKinsey, the founder of the consulting firm that still carries his name, made his early reputation as an officer in charge of logistics for the U.S. Army during the First World War[51]. Even in viscerally anti-interventionist Britain, the need to ensure strategic supplies of fuels and chemicals during the war prompted the Government to buy in 1914 a 51% of Anglo-Persian Oil (later to become British Petroleum) and to sponsor the merger during the war of a number of small British chemicals producers into a few larger firms (most notably Nobel Industries and British Dyes) which in the next decade would further consolidate into Imperial Chemical Industries (ICI)[52].

After the war, tariff protectionism, whose growth had been relatively mild before the conflict, grew dramatically around the world. Cross-border trade as a percentage of total production started to fall for the first time in over a century. Between 1913 and 1929, this ratio fell by a staggering 33% –representing an annual rate of -2.5%. The attempts by the governments of Britain, France and the USA to return to the Gold Standard proved difficult to sustain and ultimately short-lived. Just as one would expect, all this stimulated industrial concentration within national boundaries even further. In Germany, even before the Nazi Party won the elections and started to deploy its interventionist policies, the whole chemical and steel industries merged in two mammoth groups –respectively, I.G. Farben in 1925 and Vereinigte Stahlwerke in 1926. Even Britain started to move along the protectionist path (the 1915 McKenna Tariff Law representing the first departure from its formerly all-encompassing free-trade policy), and for the first time saw large mergers such as those that gave birth to ICI in 1926 or Unilever in 1929. Up to a point, U.S. antitrust legislation (most notoriously the 1890 Sherman Act) limited the extent of industrial consolidation by forcibly breaking up industrial groups whose price-setting power on the market was deemed to high, as was the case in 1911 with both Standard Oil and American Tobacco, or in 1912 with NCR. Yet, even under the pressure of this stern legal scrutiny, some notorious quasi-monopolies, such as U.S. Steel or AT&T, managed to avoid the axe for many decades.

Then, on Thursday, 24 October 1929, the New York stock market crash signalled the start of the Great Depression. Industrial production in the USA fell by nearly 50% between 1929 and 1932, and unemployment reached wholly unprecedented levels. The international markets were still global enough to spread the shock wave quickly to the rest of the world. Now, the same way protectionism reduces market uncertainty, economic crises increase it. Faced with a disaster of such proportions, governments resorted first to tariff barriers and then to the full panoply of interventionist weaponry at their disposal. Trade as a percentage of global GDP dived at a breakneck average rate of -6% a year between 1929 and 1938. Yet, of course, whether the business environment became more or less uncertain as a result of the combined impact of the crisis and of government intervention depended on the specific policies applied from country to country. At one extreme, Nazi Germany actively fostered concentration of the industrial capacity of the nation under the direct control of the State. At the other,

Roosevelt's "New Deal" policies in the U.S. belonged to a comparatively very mild brand of interventionism and thus did only partially offset the impact of the crash on business uncertainty.

The experience of the U.S. automobile industry, perhaps the most paradigmatic example of an integrated production process, constitutes an excellent example of what happened as a result. Contrary to a popular misconception, it was not the brutal fall in demand during the Great Depression that did away with the smaller American car producers like Packard, Studebaker or Hudson. Far from it. For the most part these firms survived the long crisis in remarkably good shape given the circumstances. The most successful one amid their ranks, the Chrysler Corporation, actually grew so fast throughout this period of weak, uncertain demand that, as we saw in Chapter 5, it overtook Ford to become the second largest car producer in the world. Furthermore, Chrysler achieved this precisely by retaining the structure of a medium-sized firm, rejecting vertical integration and staying flexible to respond to changes in demand through a relatively loose relationship with its suppliers, in a production process of which Chrysler only retained control over the engine build and the overall product design. Thus, by avoiding the burden of a heavy fixed cost structure like those of Ford or General Motors, it was better able to adapt to the unpredictable demand of the 1930s –whereas Ford, the most tightly integrated of the Detroit automobile producers, was the hardest hit of all. Still in 1944, as we have seen, Studebaker was regarded as a much healthier, albeit smaller, business than Ford. Thus, ironically, it was precisely when demand grew stronger and more stable as a result of the post-war boom that the smaller producers found they could not cope anymore. Already by the late 1940s, the only small American car manufacturer that was left was Willys-Overland, the producer of the famous "Jeep". Even Chrysler had to acknowledge in the late 1940s that the circumstances had changed and modify its approach in favour of a tighter, more vertically-integrated process[53].

\*\*\*\*\*

As we have seen, while an organisation following integrated mass production methods can be far more productive, under the right conditions, than the same number of people operating in separate workshops, it also requires meticulous planning and cooperation amongst the participants because, as all process components are so interdependent, any disturbance could bring the whole production chain to a halt. Centralisation consequently implies a more critical role for the manager. Thus the production process revolution, which had started impacting primarily the shop floor workers, naturally extended to the management layer above them and gave birth to the stereotype of the "man in the grey-flannel suit", the bureaucratic, intensely social organisation man of the 1940s and 50s. That this new human subspecies represented a significant change respective to its precedents was made clear by numerous observers of the period, such as David Riesman or William Whyte[54]. Whether the change was for better or worse remains of course a matter of subjective valuation –but we can only agree with Whyte that the Vicks veteran salesman who told him straight that "the man on the other side of the counter is the *enemy*" would not have sat comfortably at the General Electric young managers training program where the most important (unwritten) rule was "Never say anything controversial"[55].

Management doctrine changed accordingly. Although today we tend to regard Frederick Taylor and Henry Ford as proponents of essentially the same idea, in the early 20th Century there was a widespread acknowledgment (partially fuelled, it is true, by the two men's ego-driven rivalry) that there were significant discrepancies between their models. In this comparison, Ford's approach was often presented at the time as a more "paternalistic", less "exploitative" doctrine.[56] Few of their contemporaries, however, seem to have realised that there was an intimate link between these differences and the industries each one of these men came from. Taylor's early successes took place, after all, at steel mills, whose degree of process integration was always relatively mild compared with where the mass-production automobile plants would end up. Therefore, his approach to reducing production plant costs was aimed as much at measuring each individual contribution as at enhancing process integration.

There is an inescapable logic in this. If my cleaning lady tries to charge me more time than it logically took her to clean my home, it will be easy for me to challenge her because I, like most people, have a pretty good idea of what it takes to get her job done. But if my plumber tries to do the same, it will be much more difficult for me to argue with him, simply because his skills are much more obscure to me. Then again, if the would-be cheater is now a consultant in my team, I will be able to challenge him anyway because, complex as his skill set is, it happens to be one I understand fairly well. Therefore, if I am really concerned about the plumber's shirking at my expense (for example, because I am using his services very frequently), then my logical approach will be Taylor's: take a process chart and a stopwatch and observe him to gain the detail knowledge I am now lacking.

This is why, in Taylor's case, despite the opportunities for process rationalisation his approach uncovered, the fact that he also strongly advocated variable pay schemes based on the number of units of output produced by every individual against a standard benchmark suggests that savings were obtained as much through the minimisation of shirking opportunities as through enhanced process integration. No wonder his approach encountered so much resistance from the shop floor workers and their trade unions[57]. In Ford's production chain, conversely, this approach would just not work, for the purpose was not to have one person work any faster or slower than the other, but to keep everyone working at exactly the same pace: that of the conveyor belt. This is why he paid salaries at a flat daily rate (the famous $5 per day) and provided employee benefits that were independent of individual work effort.

This issue of the impossibility of isolating individual contributions was felt even more acutely in high-tech industries: at least Ford could police who was or was not working as instructed, whereas technology industries usually depend on tasks that appear impenetrably arcane to the uninitiated and are therefore inherently difficult to supervise. There is, in fact, probably only one type of employee whose performance is even more difficult to monitor: managers themselves –and both the Taylorite and the Fordian doctrines increasingly required armies of middle-managers/supervisors to meticulously plan and inspect the productive processes at the unprecedented scale of the new industrial giants. For this type of worker, the solution was logically to bring Ford's approach to the extreme: fixed pay, job security and overall a less uncertain work environment. It ought to be no surprise, therefore, that the "human relations" management school would have been born in the context of high-tech industries. It was under the sponsorship of Western Electric (the manufacturing arm of AT&T) that Elton Mayo conducted his famous experiments on employee motivation in the 1930s; and it was at General Electric where the first modern young managers training programmes were put in place.

Within this context, the history of IBM during the long tenure of its first chairman, Thomas J. Watson, Sr. (1914-1956) constitutes a case in point. Far from being the near-monopoly of mainframe computers it later became, in the first half of the 20th Century IBM was a producer of precision machines, ranging from cash registers to typewriters, which played on a level field against similarly-sized competitors like NCR, Burroughs or Honeywell. In the 1930s, however, the company differentiated itself from its competitors by its willingness to "buffer out" market risk away from its employees and thus provide them with a more stable, less uncertain work environment. As the Great Depression deepened and its competitors cut back sharply their employee numbers, the IBM leadership team decided to keep employment intact among the ranks. Furthermore, in 1936 the company did away with the traditional pay incentives for lower-skill workers, based on units produced, that constituted the norm among its competitors and, instead, instituted a straight salary per worker. The somewhat counter-intuitive result of this policy was that output per worker increased, and IBM's market positioning jumped ahead of its competitors. As Peter Drucker (who witnessed how the firm operated in those days) described it in 1954:

"As a result [of these measures] IBM workers are not afraid of 'working themselves out of a job'. They do not restrict their output. They do not resent it if one of their fellow-workers produces more; after all, this will neither result in a higher output norm for themselves nor endanger their job security. And they do not resist change."

In other words: by reducing the level of uncertainty its workers were subject to, IBM created a more cooperative environment –and this translated into measurable results.

From this viewpoint, it is interesting that the "human relations" management school Elton Mayo initiated in the 1930s, and later Abraham Maslow and Douglas McGregor[58] developed in the 1950s and 60s, would have been presented as a radical departure from the "scientific management" tradition of Taylor and Ford –for it actually was, to a large extent, its logical continuation. The same way Ford's $5 flat daily rates and generous employee benefits were a logical response to a system where lack of cooperation was more dangerous than in Taylor's steelworks, so was the heavy emphasis on a "friendly" work environment that the human relations school borrowed from high-tech industries a sensible response to an environment where shirking was even more difficult to police. In other words: if, following McGregor's terminology, we define "Theory X" as the doctrine that regards supervision, reward and punishment as the most effective management tools, whereas "Theory Y" is the view that it is better to provide people with an inspirational environment, then, as shirking became more difficult to monitor, Theory X would just have become less effective. The levers to behaviour control whose usage the human management school advocated had always existed, to be sure –only, as their alternatives lost their effectiveness, the human relations tools turned more attractive by default.

This is why it was in the forties and fifties when the personnel departments of America's largest corporations started the practice of systematically screening out candidates not only on the basis of their technical skills but also of their social proficiency –what was then described as the "well-rounded man" profile[59]. When it is difficult to measure objective results because everyone depends on everyone else, it makes more sense to rate people on the basis of their attitude instead. This is also why, over time, even Mr. Richardson, the Vicks executive we introduced in Chapter 2, ended up having to change his mind. According to Whyte, by the mid-1950s he was still heading the young managers' school, but the name had changed to "The Vicks Executive Development Program" and, while the old "survival of the fittest" ideology had not (yet) completely faded away, there was now a much heavier emphasis on development of "soft" management skills (as opposed to "on the road" sales experience), and all but a handful of the trainees could expect to find a permanent job at Vicks at the end of the programme.

By 1950, the capitalist world orbited unambiguously around the United States, where, in turn, most of the core industries were dominated by a small set of very large players. In industrial economics, scale and scope were unanimously regarded as the twin cornerstones of superior performance. In political economy, Keynesian interventionism was rampant everywhere. Even more spectacularly, beyond the "Iron Curtain" a good third of humanity lived under communist regimes that stood as the very paradigm of centralisation. Despite the recent defeat of the fascist Axis, social planning and industrial consolidation seemed to be where the future lay... Yet the tide of History was about to turn.

# 7.  THE TURN OF THE TIDE

*"And it is just as true in politics as it is in any art or craft: new methods must drive out old ones. When a city can live in peace and quiet, no doubt the old established ways are best; but when one is constantly being faced by new problems, one has also to be capable of approaching them in an original way."*[*]

- Thucydides, *The Peloponnesian War*

In the mid-1950s, just as William Whyte denounced the weakening of the old "protestant ethic" and Peter Drucker thundered against bureaucratic capitalism and stated that "so much of what we call management consists of making it difficult for people to work", the pendulum of History was starting to swing the other way. Slowly at first, after the end of World War II the economies of the industrialised world began to liberalise again, in a process that has essentially kept gaining momentum until today. By 1950, the global ratio of trade as a percentage of GDP had climbed back to its 1929 level; by the early 1970s, it surpassed its 1913 peak for the first time[60]. We have already talked at length about what this has done to the global business environment in Chapters 1 and 2 –but now we are in a better position to understand why. Graphically, we could represent the market's move to a more uncertain, competitive environment as the A→B solid arrow on Figure 4:

---

[*] Translation by Rex Warner.

**Figure 4**

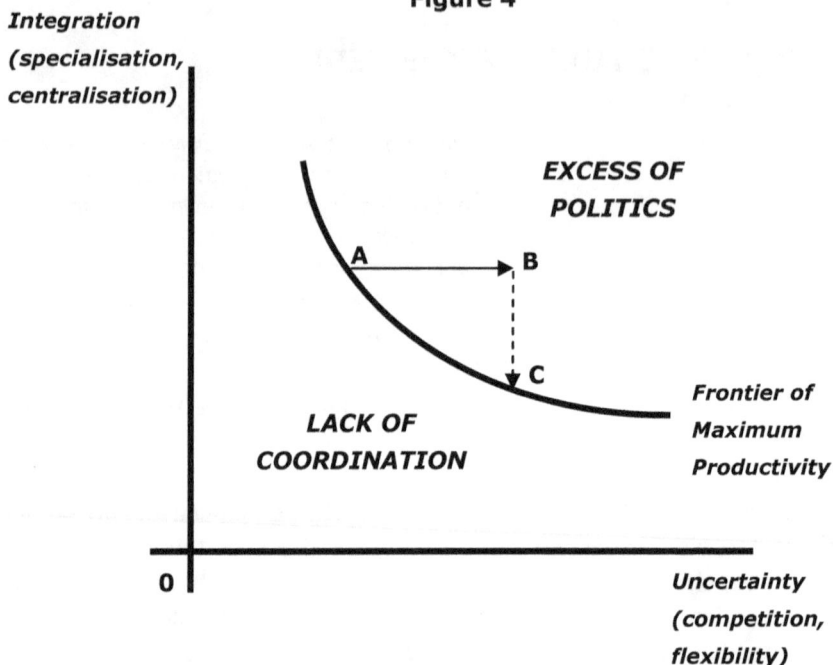

To be sure, the ideal approach for an organisation under these conditions would be to decentralise following the dotted arrow B→C. Yet this type of move, as we already know, is bound to generate resistance precisely from those who benefit the most from a centralised system –who are often also the people that hold the power to decide whether the change will take place or not. The organisation thus becomes much more intensely political, but a long time can pass until the consequences become unmistakably reflected on the accounting bottom line. How long? As we have seen, examples like Marks & Spencer or the Ford Motor Co. suggest that fifteen or twenty years between the commission of the original sin and the day of reckoning are by no means unheard of –and this, in our fast-paced times, feels like a long time indeed.

Hence, just as one would have expected, the intensification of competition that came along with the process of globalisation created a general demand for "flexibility" (rated now far above the old requirement for "discipline") and a slowly but consistently increasing corporate focus on the short term. True to form, at first most large corporations responded to the challenge by doing more of the same, i.e., by seeking even larger economies of scale and scope. Thus, in Chandler's words, "by the late 1960s the drive for growth through acquisition and merger had almost become a mania."[61] The number of Merger and Acquisition (M&A) operations in the USA soared from 2,125 in 1965 to 6,107 in 1969, and in most cases the only stated objective of these operations was the weakest form of synergy: diversification. According to Chandler, from 1963 to 1972 almost three quarters of the assets acquired were for product diversification, and half of these were in unrelated products: in other words, corporations were trying to use product scope to hedge their bets against an increasingly uncertain market. As a result, average firm size increased: between 1963 and 1967, the percentage of people working for firms of 10,000 or more employees went up from 24.9% to 28.1% in the USA[62].

Only, this soon proved to be a counterproductive approach: in a winner-take-all market, focus is a virtue, and trying to compete in all the specialties is a sure way to lose every single race. The market has a particularly brutal way to highlight corporate mistakes, and this instance was not an exception. Thus, when the combined shock of the dollar collapse and the oil price increase in 1971-73 brought the world economy to its knees and, as economic crises always do, pushed the level of business uncertainty still further up, the acquisition fever paused and then reversed. In 1971 there were only 4,608 M&A operations in the USA, in 1974 just 2,861, and from 1974 to 1977 there was one divestiture for every two mergers or acquisitions –a ratio that had been one to eleven in 1965. Slowly and painfully, during the recession of the seventies the message finally sank in: the rules of the game had changed. Scale and scope did not hold the key to superior efficiency anymore: in fact, trying to extend a firm's scope beyond its core skills and thus gain economies of scale and hedge market-specific risks was now increasingly regarded as a losing strategy.

*In Search of Excellence*, the 1982 bestseller by Tom Peters and Robert Waterman, echoed the new sentiment[63]. On the basis on their observations over a sample of successful companies in the USA, these authors advised firms to foster "autonomy and entrepreneurship" within their organisations by "breaking the corporation into small companies and encouraging them to think independently and competitively", and also to "stick to the knitting", that is, to "remain with the business the company knows best". These are all recommendations that 19th Century British entrepreneurs might easily have subscribed to, but would not have sat very well with the apostles of scientific management of the first half of the 20th Century. The process of decentralisation continued unabated. The eighties saw the fever of Leveraged Buy-Outs (LBO's), where large, inefficient corporations were bought up and then resold in separate pieces whose total market value happened to be higher than that of the original, integrated firm. In a way, this was the exact opposite of the M&A wave of the late sixties, and had just the opposite effect: from 1977 to 1992, the percentage of people working for firms of 10,000 or more employees fell from 28% to 24.4% in the USA[64]. At the same time, downsizing waves followed one another, cutting deep into the middle-management hierarchy layers while significantly curtailing the power grip of worker unions. The social impact of these changes cannot be underestimated, particularly in the USA: in the ten years from 1979 to 1989, the *Fortune 100* firms lost 1.5 million employees, or 14% of the total workforce[65].

In this context, a number of large industrial holdings managed to survive and thrive, but only to the extent they reproduced the market's dynamics within themselves. This explains why the policy of remaining only in those markets where it could be the first or second player worked so well for General Electric when its CEO, Jack Welch, started to apply it in the 1980s. In a highly competitive, winner-take-all market there is not glory (or profit) in being an also-ran, and by staying put under these conditions a corporation is effectively subsidising non-profitable businesses at the expense of profitable ones. As the same ruthless market logic extended to the firm's human resource policies, it translated into a drastic reduction of GE's total workforce[66] from 400,000 to 300,000 between 1982 and 1985, and won for Welch the highly descriptive nickname of "Neutron Jack". After this initial shake-up, GE adopted its famous "rank and yank" annual performance review policy, which routinely results in the dismissal of the bottom 10-20% performers every 2-3 years. Later, other large corporations in trouble followed a similar path to recovery. In the nineties, for example, John Browne (later Lord Browne) applied a similar type of medicine to BP, which had been brought to the brink of collapse by the toughened market conditions that followed the dramatic oil price dive in the mid-eighties. Scores of staff workers were laid off, large parts of the business were outsourced, and the prevalent working style became a lot more entrepreneurial and less bureaucratic. In only a few years, the ailing company had been turned around to become the fastest-growing of the oil super-majors.

Eventually the academia got the message too and proceeded to dig out factual evidence to explain these phenomena. In 1995, a groundbreaking paper [67] found that diversified companies were valued by the U.S. stock market at a discount of between 13% and 15% respective to the imputed individual value of their parts. Yet, at the same time, the same type of evidence indicates also that this "diversification discount" did not exist until the late seventies[68], and that in less liberal economies like the U.K. or Japan it is still significantly smaller than in the USA[69]. In other words: scale and scope may no longer represent the source of competitive advantage they used to be, but this does not contradict the fact that, until the seventies, they did. Thus, as it happens, the same way Taylor and Ford presented their ideas as universal truths akin to gravitation force, when their applicability was actually bound to a time and a place, so do our modern management gurus all too often seem to forget that their advice is only valid under a given set of circumstances that have been different in the past and might change again in the future.

\*\*\*\*\*

IBM in the 1980s constitutes a particularly interesting example of a company under this type of shock. Until the mid-1980s, IBM was a widely admired market leader that Peters and Waterman did not hesitate to place at a particularly pre-eminent spot amid their "excellent companies". By the late eighties, however, the computer industry had experienced a dramatic transformation and, with the arrival of new challengers like Intel, Oracle or Microsoft, had become much more aggressively competitive. "Big Blue", accustomed to milking the near-monopoly of the mainframe computer market it had enjoyed since it launched its epoch-making System/360 (or "S/360") in 1964, simply could not cope with this drastic surge in its exposure to market uncertainty.

At the time of its inception, S/360 was the result of an extremely bold initiative championed by the chairman, Thomas J. Watson, Jr. – the son of the same Thomas J. Watson, Sr. whose personnel policies we discussed in the previous chapter. The total development cost of this revolutionary mainframe system was an astronomic five billion U.S. dollars of the day (almost $30 billion of today). Watson famously remarked in his memoirs that it was more expensive than the Manhattan Project that built the first A-bomb[70], and *Fortune Magazine* referred to the project at the time as IBM's "$5 billion gamble". IBM certainly bet the farm on this venture: it almost wrecked the finances of the firm, and it would probably have been abandoned long before the end had the chairman not stood so firmly behind it, or the development team not been so committed to the task. Yet, as soon as it was commercialised, it became a wild success. IBM received over a thousand orders for S/360s just in the first 30 days after its launch on 7 April 1964. The system was technically and operationally so far ahead of any alternative product that the competition could produce, that IBM soon held a virtual monopoly of the mainframe market –and retained it for nearly a quarter of a century.

By the late 1980s, however, when a new technology generation changed the rules of the game again and Big Blue found itself thrown back into the competitive pit again, it found that, throughout its long years of unchallenged success, it had grown overweight. It had become just too big, too bureaucratic and, under this new pressure, increasingly way too political to be able to fight this battle successfully. Its customer service, which in 1982 was one of the aspects of the organisation Peters and Waterman had most warmly commended in their book, only a few years thereafter became widely regarded as poor, arrogant and outrageously expensive. Nearly all analysts, journalists and consultants recommended the same: to slim down the firm and break it down into smaller pieces (i.e., in our Figure 4, to drastically slide down the B→C arrow). For several painful years, the leadership team under CEO John Akers tried, with variable degrees of conviction, to head in that direction –but, just as one would expect, this was a bit like asking the passengers of a plane to choose who is going to be thrown out so that the others can survive. Between 1990 and 1993, the company abandoned its old lifetime employment policy and laid off well over 100,000 employees, over a quarter of its workforce –but the main result was deeper uncertainly, office politics and internal chaos. As a consequence, performance worsened instead of improving. From February 1991 to the end of 1992, the total market value of the firm plummeted from $139.50 billion to only $50.38 billion –an astonishing drop of nearly 65% in less than two years[71]. By this time, the company was not only making huge losses (in 1993 it reported a record loss of $8.1 billion), but also faced the distinct possibility of having to file for bankruptcy within a year. Hence, when a new CEO, Lou Gerstner, was appointed in 1993, his first and most urgent task was to stop the bleeding and raise cash to the extent required to save the business[72].

In many aspects, Gerstner followed the approach most of the analysts and the economic press were recommending. This certainly includes the sales of non-core assets (primarily driven by the imperative to raise cash), further headcount reductions (in 1993-94 the headcount was cut down by a further 80,000, about a 27% of the workforce) and the extensive introduction of variable compensation schemes. Against the opinions expressed by a significant portion of the financial journals, however, his approach was to keep the company in a single piece. Instead of breaking it up, his team found a way to move it into a different business space (primarily centred on IT-related services of integration and outsourcing) where competition was not (yet?) so brutal and scale still represented a significant advantage. In short: the key behind IBM's turnaround was to move the company into a related business where its structure and size still allowed it to play at an advantage. The percentage represented by services on the total revenue of the firm thus climbed up from 25% in 1992 to nearly 43% in 2001, even before its acquisition of Price Waterhouse Coopers (PwC) Consulting in October 2002, which turned Big Blue into the largest consulting firm worldwide.

In the process, IBM may indeed have become somewhat nimbler and more dynamic, but for the most part it is still the large, heavily bureaucratic organisation it used to be –as evidenced by the steady exodus of ex-PwC consultants that have been leaving the organisation for the last few years. When asked, these individuals typically explain that they leave because they find the IBM environment intolerably bureaucratic, at least compared with the one they knew at PwC when it was still part of a professional partnership. Whether or for how long the market space that IBM occupies today will remain friendly to its organisation model, and whether the appearance of low-cost service providers like Indian-based Wipro or Tata will change the rules of the game away from Big Blue's comfort zone remains, of course, still to be seen. At the time of writing these lines (summer of 2005), however, IBM's recently issued profit warning and its decision to drastically cut back on headcount at a global level seems to suggest that History may well be repeating itself.

*****

A remarkable phenomenon that reinforces this interpretation of the impact of intensified global competition on the business environment is the superior performance of family firms observed throughout the last few years in the USA. Family-controlled businesses are nearly always less meritocratic than their competitors, if nothing else because appointment to the top positions is usually based on family connections rather than true merit. We have already seen, in the case of Marks & Spencer, how the transition to a more meritocratic environment had a significant impact on the internal dynamics of the firm as a whole. So, if the processes of the average company of our days are indeed too integrated for its levels of internal meritocracy, we should expect its performance to be worse than that of the average family-controlled company within the same economic space. This is exactly what has been found in a number of recent studies. In 2003, for instance, a research paper[73] based on the performance of a sample of S&P 500 companies from 1992 to 1999 came to the conclusion that in the U.S. not only "family firms are significantly better performers than non-family firms," but also that "the greater profitability in family firms, relative to non-family, stems from those firms in which a family member serves as the CEO." The authors even found that there is an "optimal" degree of family-control, as "performance is first increasing and then decreasing in ownership [...]. In other words, when families have the greatest control of the firm, the potential for entrenchment and poor performance is the greatest." Several authors[74] suggest that U.S. family firms today are able to attain greater investment efficiency due to their longer investment horizons. Conversely, in less liberal economies such as the ones in East Asia, the same type of evidence[75] indicates that family ownership tends to hamper performance. Indeed, the very fact that family ownership is commonly perceived to be associated to poor performance in the USA suggests that the conditions have probably changed since the days when these conceptions were first developed and popularised.

How do the internal dynamics of a family firm differ from those of a publicly-traded one? I would like to illustrate it with an example from my own personal experience. Early in my career, I worked as an internal auditor at the headquarters of a large Spanish holding, a leader of the consumer goods sector in that country. The group was organised and managed almost as a personal asset portfolio of the controlling family. The president of the holding company was the eldest son of the deceased founder, while his younger brother occupied a divisional director position whose content no one seemed to clearly understand. In practice, the firm was run, fairly autocratically, by quite a capable Director General who had been the right hand of the founder since the days when the current president was a baby. Under him, however, the quality of the rest of the core leadership team was fairly uneven. In fact, the firm's criteria for career advancement did not seem to be so much linked to demonstrated "performance" and capability (although these were evidently important factors) as to length of tenure and to a certain old-fashioned concept of "loyalty".

Yet the system, in defiance of some of the best respected schools of management thought, worked extremely well. Every three or four years, the group would start up a handful of new businesses in areas more or less related to the group's core skills, with the expectation that perhaps one of them would do awesomely, one would do awfully, and the remaining two or three would probably fall somewhere in between. For each one of these new businesses, they would set up a different legal entity (sometimes a joint venture with a franchiser) and preferably put in place a leadership team detached from the gilded ranks of trusted insiders at the headquarters. The point was that, even if the business went badly, or if they decided to sell it off, the group would not, under normal circumstances, spare any effort to retrieve these managers and redeploy them somewhere else within the holding. Furthermore, contrary to the normal policy of so many publicly-traded corporations, the group would actually prefer to hire, when given the choice, relatives of its current and past employees rather than complete strangers. The organisation, in other words, did not fear nepotism: in a way, nepotism was one of the pillars of the system –a bit like in a family. The upside was of course that, in this environment of reduced uncertainty, there was more room for internal cooperation. The downside was that employees who started with no blood or friendship ties to the upper *échelons* of the hierarchy could only reasonably expect a slow-paced career, and would therefore be tempted to leave and test themselves in the wider world –just as I did myself. One could say that this holding was, in many respects, a bit like a Japanese firm.

*****

As a matter of fact, it could be argued that Japanese companies in the eighties performed a role very similar to the one German firms had played almost a century before. Much has been made of the alleged superiority of Confucian values to explain the higher productivity of Nippon factories but, whatever the merits of this argument, cultural differences alone cannot explain the consistently superior performance of Japanese plants located in the U.S. and staffed with American employees. And the difference is significant. For example, according to an estimate, in the 1980s Japanese firms in the United States operating under the Japanese management system produced approximately 30% more gross output per person than their American-owned counterparts[76]. Another study, this time focused specifically on the automobile industry[77], pointed out that in those years American-owned production plants in the USA spent an average of 24.9 man-hours per vehicle, whereas the equivalent figure for US-based Japanese plants was a mere 20.9. The technology, the type of resources and the cultural background of most of the people employed in those plants was essentially the same as in their US-owned rivals: the productivity gap was primarily due to a different management system.

Yet the fact is that the key components of the Japanese system (long-term employment, tenure-based promotions, emphasis on discipline and cooperation) would have felt quite familiar to the American organisation men of the 1940s and 50s. When one reads Whyte's testimony that most of the young organisation men in the

1950s really seemed to believe in the maxim of "be loyal to the company and the company will be loyal to you" (which, incidentally, baffled him almost as much as it now baffles us), one cannot help thinking that the same would equally apply to most Japanese middle managers of the 1980s. Simply put, Japanese companies in the 1970s and 80s were less aggressively meritocratic than their American competitors, and this, while imposing on them the price of suboptimal selection for promotion through the perversities of the "Peter Principle", also fostered cooperation and thus ultimately made a highly integrated production system possible –which, as we have seen, translated into measurably higher productivity.

The parallels with the British-German commercial rivalry in the 1880s are startling indeed. Just like the early German industrialists, the Japanese were conquering the world from the platform of a home market fiercely protected by trade barriers, legal constraints and cultural idiosyncrasies, whereas their American rivals contended from the basis of a more open economy and a more diverse society. Large Japanese groups (the *keiretsu*) raised most of their capital on the basis of their close association to credit institutions, in a dynamic that in the Anglo-Saxon world would be regarded as nearly incestuous, if not blatantly corrupt. American companies, instead, had to rely on the liquidity provided by a much more transparent financial market that tended to demand more immediate, tangible results. The paradoxical consequence was that American managers had to discount their investment decisions at a much higher rate than their Asian competitors –or, what is the same, to focus much more heavily on the short run. A paper by James Poterba and Lawrence Summers[78] based on interviews with American CEOs found that "at the time of the survey, the fall of 1990, U.S. CEOs believed that their firms had systematically shorter time horizons than their major competitors in Europe and (especially) Asia." Thus, for a while, American companies were like the marathon runner that wastes all his energies in the first few metres and then, exhausted, has to drag himself to the end line while his competitors speed ahead.

If imitation is the sincerest form of flattery, then the eighties were doubtlessly Japan's glory years. Alarmed by their country's loss of competitive edge, a long procession of American managers and scholars flocked to the Land of the Rising Sun hoping to unveil its competitive secrets and bring them back to the USA. Yet, as a matter of fact, this otherwise sensible strategy, while often yielding valuable results when focused on the adoption of specific, well-defined techniques (e.g., Just-In-Time inventory management, or later Total Quality Management), tended to fail when applied at a grander scale. Perhaps the most famous instance of this type of failure is General Motors' unsuccessful attempt in the 1980s to install and efficiently operate automated plants like those of its Japanese rivals. In a titanic effort to achieve this, the company spent a breathtaking $62.8 billion in Research & Development (R&D) between 1980 and 1990 –which was hailed by many financial analysts as a bold move to reverse the chronic lack of investment that they perceived as the main cause of America's competitive disadvantage. Yet, after all this monumental spending, by 1990 GM's total equity value was a mere $20.8 billion, and its production process was still so uncompetitive that it generated losses of $6.5 billion in the following two years[79]. One cannot help thinking that all this R&D money would have been much better invested if it had simply been kept in the proverbial shoebox.

The reason for these expensive flops was already evident to Marvin Harris[80] in 1981 as he wrote that "the main problem as the American consumer sees it is not that Japan has risen to industrial pre-eminence but that the quality of American-made goods seems to have deteriorated. In concentrating on finding out why the Japanese have beaten them, American managers may be running away from the more important question of why they let U.S. product quality decline." Thus, in the end, apart from their renewed emphasis on "teamwork" (which actually was no novelty at all), American companies found that it was more productive for them not to imitate the management methods of their Japanese rivals but, instead, to deepen and leverage their decentralization to gain the higher ground. Thus, in terms of our Figure 4, having found themselves at point B, the solution was not to try to swim against the tide and move back to the left of the diagram (i.e., back to point A), but rather to reorganise in a more decentralised structure and thus slide down following the B→C arrow. In the process, scores of middle-management positions were downsized and "takeover sharks" hunted down oversize corporate whales to rip them apart –but then again, attrition wars are never a pretty sight.

The key difference between the 1880s and the 1980s is that, although the frozen picture may look so strikingly similar at first glance, the pendulum of History was swinging in the opposite direction in one case versus the other. As we have seen above, from 1870 to 1945 the whole world moved slowly but inexorably away from globalisation. Since 1945, it has been moving with equal sense of inevitability towards it. Thus, while the industrial might of Germany grew so much in the 19th Century that it nearly defeated the combined forces of the rest of Europe in two world wars, the Japanese system of the 1970s led to a monumental financial bubble from whose collapse in 1991 the Nippon economy has not yet been able to recover. It is now the highly conservative, protectionist, bureaucratic Japanese system the one that is under overwhelming pressure to change and to adapt its investment horizons to what our global, competitive, impatient markets demand. For, whether it is in Asia or Europe or America, the business environment is anything but static –and, particularly for the last thirty years, it has been moving with increasing speed towards globalisation... Which means that companies constantly need to adapt to an ever-more-uncertain framework and, until they do so, or while they explore all the apparently less painful solutions, they find themselves in the "excess of politics" quadrant in Figure 4 –in other words, in Dilbert's world.

# 8. POWER, APPEARANCES AND THE FLIGHT FROM RESPONSIBILITY

> *"**Power Mist:** The tendency of hierarchies in office environments to be diffuse and preclude crisp articulation."*
>
> - Douglas Coupland, *Generation X*

In February 1942, the island stronghold of Singapore, which the British High Command had repeatedly described as "unassailable", fell to the Japanese Army in the course of an invasion that went so quickly from first landing to unconditional surrender that even the Nippon commanders were staggered. In the event, 138,708 British, Indian and Australian soldiers either died or went into captivity, and control of the strategic Strait of Malacca changed hands. History remembers today the Fall of Singapore not only as one of the most shattering disasters ever experienced by the British Army but also, and perhaps above all, as a major example of the effects of military incompetence. Political jockeying across the British Army, the Navy and the Air Force throughout the 1920s and 1930s resulted in the defences of the island being designed under outdated concepts and with very little consideration for an overall strategy. At the time of the invasion, the Supreme Commander of the British Forces in Malacca was Lieutenant General Percival. In his lucid analysis of the psychology of military incompetence, Norman Dixon[81] tells us that Percival "was in fact highly intelligent, and had shown himself in previous years to be a brilliant staff officer." Yet the qualities required for success as a staff officer at the Army High Command, like at the headquarters of any large, bureaucratic organisation, are completely different from those required to lead an army on the field. It would be long and ultimately pointless to try to list here all the absurd mistakes that were made by the British commanders in the course of this campaign, and that led to such a quick defeat. The common denominator of the most astonishing of them, however, was an obsessive focus on appearances at the expense of the real issues at hand. Dixon, for instance, recounts the following scene between Percival and a subordinate, Brigadier Simson, who was trying to obtain permission to build defences against the Japanese attack that was about to fall on them:

> "Hence it is a measure of the seriousness with which Brigadier Simson regarded the situation that he made one last attempt to move his general"…"The plea was forceful, respectful and logical but, amazingly, the general remained unmoved. Simson, his anger rising, said: 'Look here, General —I've raised this question time after time. You've always refused. What's more, you've always refused to give me any *reasons*. At least tell me one thing —why on earth *are* you taking this stand?' At long last the General Officer Commanding Malaya gave his answer. 'I believe that defences of the sort you want to throw up are bad for the morale of troops and civilians.'"…"Simson was 'frankly horrified' and remembers standing there in the room suddenly feeling quite cold, and realizing that, except for a miracle, Singapore was as good as lost. As he put on his Sam Browne, Simson could not forebear to make one last remark – 'Sir, it's going to be much worse for morale if the Japanese start running all over the island.'"

Dixon concluded from this and other case studies that this focus on appearances is key to understand the most spectacular instances of crass incompetence in the armed forces. But why? He found the answer in the fact that the conditions for success in bureaucratic institutions such as the Army drive military leaders to become "social rather than task specialists". For, in an institution where promotion is at least partially based on merit, incompetence cannot be an accident: as Andrew Gordon[82] incisively pointed out, "every proven military incompetent has previously displayed attributes which his superiors rewarded."

Poor business management rarely, if ever, leads to such dire consequences; but, once we have allowed for this difference in degree, it is easy to see that General Percival is a close relative of the executives whose motto seems to be "let nothing stick to you". This is by no means a coincidence. Just like Percival, modern managers are exposed to an environment that is much more uncertain than the one their organisations were designed for, and their reactions are thus essentially the same as those of a staff officer with well-honed social skills who would suddenly be sent to lead a platoon under fire. And just as Brigadier Simson could not understand how such an intelligent man could behave so stupidly, many employees of large organisations feel today tempted to believe that there must indeed be a "Dilbert Principle" at work such that idiots are regularly promoted to management above their more capable peers.

For we should never forget that he who occupies a position of privilege knows only too well that he is being rewarded above the real value of his skills: this is, after all, the very definition of privilege. He or she remains in that position to a large extent because the rest of the organisation somehow agrees to it, and this in turn happens because those who are less privileged have not (yet?) found a way to bump him out of that comfortable armchair. What justifies the privilege is the asymmetric information carried by the position, that is, put simply, the fact that the privileged leader is better informed about his team than the other way around. Thus, the key to retaining the privilege is controlling the flows of information, and this means making sure that one's appearance is beyond any possible criticism, that nothing happens without one knowing it and that the roles of one's subordinates are so narrowly defined that none of them has a clear view of the full picture. Also, if at all possible, the astute bureaucrat will try to distribute responsibilities among his subordinates so that they feel they have to compete against each other in order to gain the leader's favour – which will logically compel them to withhold information from each other while whispering about each other's weaknesses at the leader's ear. This is how the self-serving manager so often becomes a bottleneck instead of an accelerator for decision making, a dark hole instead of a light reflector to diffuse relevant information, and a

EDUARD GRACIA

breeder of conflict instead of cooperation among the members of his
team.

The individual entrepreneur cares little about appearances unless
they have a direct impact on tangible results, for it is these that
define for him the difference between success and failure. Yet in a
centralised organisation individual responsibilities are diffuse, and
therefore upward management becomes more critical for career
advancement than proficiency at execution. This drives the focus
towards appearances and away from the tasks at hand. Indeed, I
have frequently observed that those people at management
positions who claim to focus only on the "big picture" and not to
have the time for execution details are, very often, almost obsessed
with another sort of detail, such as the type of tie that combines with
a given suit or the colour patterns on a PowerPoint presentation slide
–in other words, cosmetic details that would be relevant for a social
rather than a task specialist. Under pressure, these managers will
react by doing more of the same: struggling for political positioning,
avoiding responsibility and manipulating the people around them.
This is why corporate mission/vision statements have become such a
sad joke –for it is precisely in those organisations that are under the
heaviest pressure and therefore need most urgently a clear direction
where we usually see the blandest, emptiest, most manipulative
vision statements. The prestige of mission/vision statements has
fallen so low that, when in 1993 Lou Gerstner, at his first press
conference after becoming IBM's new CEO, tried to express the need
to abandon blue-sky babble and focus on the tasks at hand, he
famously stated that "the last thing IBM needs right now is a
vision."[83]

*****

Now we should be in the position to better understand the
managerial attitudes that we found so puzzling in Chapter 2. It is the
increased competitive pressure that has led to a faster job
turnaround in management positions. However, as organisations
present rigidity towards changes in their internal structure, the

short-term focus induced by this pressure translates into more intense internal politics aimed by the players at securing for themselves a place among the privileged few –i.e., into a starker Prisoner's Dilemma. In this more aggressively competitive world, one should also expect to find a lower incidence of the Peter Principle, because promotion would tend to be granted on the basis of demonstrated capability to perform at the higher position –as opposed to past performance against the specific challenges of the lower position, let alone straight length of tenure. The old promotion rules, based on a combination of tenure, demonstrated loyalty and performance at the original role, which caused people to be "promoted to their maximum level of incompetence" were there not because top management in those days could not think of anything better, but simply because they preserved peace in their organisations. Yet today, as the surrounding market pressure increases, organisations are being pushed towards the right side of Figure 4 and, until they learn to give up some of the synergies they used to enjoy, they are exposed to seeing internal politics consume as much time and energy as these synergies produce –and then some.

An organisation that has thus moved towards the right hand side of the maximum productivity frontier, as in point B in Figure 4, but not changed its internal processes will maintain the emphasis on teamwork (i.e., on cooperation) that Riesman and Whyte already witnessed in full force in the 1940s and 50s. Nonetheless, as promotions will now be more competitive, they will also be less driven by tenure and more by networking and communication skills, for these are, we like it or not, typically more critical abilities at the higher levels in the organisation. As the reward for sustained loyalty is thus reduced, however, there is a strong incentive for people to divert their efforts towards gaining visibility and demonstrating those communication skills that will enhance their chances of promotion, as opposed to getting the "real work" done –especially as, in a team work environment, it can be quite difficult to identify exactly what each one's contribution really was. Thus, even if people cooperate and do not sabotage each other's work (which is at best an optimistic assumption), when the stakes in this "internal tournament" are high enough the logical result is that all-too-common team environment where everyone is trying to grab bits of "leadership" glory and no one wants to perform the hands-on tasks that ultimately are the key for the team as a whole to succeed.

At the same time, it is not always clear that this meritocratic tournament will always result in the promotion of the best candidates either, for it can also trigger unintended consequences. To begin with, the skills required to ensure visibility for one's own accomplishments (at the expense of everyone else's if necessary) are not necessarily those that would ensure successful completion of the duties, supervisory or not, associated to the higher position. Maybe even more critically, the best strategy for each individual player will logically be to focus not only on enhancing one's own promotion profile but also on undermining the prospects of precisely those objectively best qualified among their rivals (for, what sense would it make to waste one's poison on a rival that is hopeless anyway?). This of course will frequently result in mediocre candidates being promoted above their better qualified colleagues. Indeed, to the extent mediocre candidates are, by definition, a majority, the chances of the best candidates falling off the competition under the sniping of their less gifted colleagues become, other things being equal, very high. Under these conditions, a superior candidate's most rational strategy will be to invest a further portion of his or her effort (in addition to what has already been devoted to enhance visibility and to demonstrate the skills required at higher levels) to counter these political manoeuvres with similar political weapons: establishing the right alliances, taking other people's credit, avoiding responsibility, bad-mouthing potential rivals and so on.

Both the mediocre and the superior manager will thus try to avoid the risks of responsibility and stick instead to the role of a neutral communicator. As Richard Sennett[84] describes this all-too-common character:

"He is a manager of process. His job, facilitation and mediation, can be, with enough savoir faire, divorced from outcome. The word 'leader' thus hardly applies to him in the traditional sense of authority."

Managers who drift along while letting "nothing stick" to them are thus by no means exceptional, because they have genuinely good reasons to behave in this fashion. As a result, this type of system will frequently lead to the promotion of candidates who, capable or not, display a marked aversion to personal accountability, but who at the same time are masters in the art of managing appearances and communication.

Indeed –if I may allow myself a personal digression at this point– this is one of the main differences in management style I observed when, in late 1996, I moved from Barcelona (a more traditional business environment largely dominated by small-to-medium, often family-owned companies) to New York to work for a consultancy. For me, the whole experience was particularly illuminating because having been raised in such a different environment made the contrasts feel starker –a bit like travelling fast forward on the time machine. In America, managers displayed less of a distant attitude, smiled a lot more and insisted on being addressed more informally. Their personal appearance was a lot more casual (at many companies ties were literally nowhere to be seen) but also, intriguingly, a lot more carefully crafted –in fact, I soon learned that the well-groomed, young-looking, narcissistic manager was more than a stereotype. Business language had become so mild that even the word "problem" seemed too strong and tended to be replaced by "issue" –which, in turn, was already starting to feel too strong a word as well, and was therefore more and more often being replaced by "challenge" or simply "situation". Worker infractions that, in a more traditional environment, would have made a manager roar to restore discipline, in America seemed to be but a trigger for the team leader to have a friendly, almost psychoanalytic counselling session with the offender.

Sure enough, under this velvety cloak, hierarchical power was still there all the same –but its expression was a lot less evident to the untrained eye. The wording of performance reviews, for example, was often so cryptic that mentors trying to gather evidence on individuals' performance would routinely have to call the reviewers directly to clarify what they *really* meant to say –which of course defeated the purpose of the written review. In other words, in their zeal to avoid situations of confrontation, managers would often avoid providing unambiguous feedback about an individual's performance to the interested person. The very definition of "leadership skills" seemed to have changed: leadership was no longer about setting a clear direction and, well, leading the troops along the way, but about facilitation, gentle persuasion and consensus-building skills –in short, seductiveness instead of statesmanship. The emphasis was consequently placed on social skills ("team play") and flexibility. One sometimes had the impression that not even the accusation of underperformance was really as damaging as that of not being a team player. These priorities may seem upside-down, at least from a more traditional viewpoint, but there is an inescapable logic in them: for a management system that requires team consensus to rule, attitudes conducive to shatter this consensus are much more dangerous than individual lack of productivity.

It would be unfair to convey a pejorative image of participatory management as a principle. There is absolutely nothing wrong with, and a lot to be said for, facilitation and consensus-building skills. They doubtlessly constitute vital skills in a decentralised environment, where gentle persuasion often needs to take the place of command and control –and, particularly in a highly uncertain business environment, there is also a lot to be said in favour of decentralisation. I, for one, would find it very difficult to go back and adapt to the authoritarian, despotic, status-conscious management style that dominates traditional business environments. Nonetheless, when the process is tightly integrated, the ownership for specific outcomes is inherently ambiguous –and, when the risk of a decision is high, so is the temptation to hide behind this ambiguity.

\*\*\*\*\*

How damaging can this temptation be? What is wrong, after all, with managers being primarily facilitators or, as business gurus so often preach, "coaches"? When Douglas McGregor, perhaps the most representative member of the "human relations" management school, tried to apply his own theories to his role as President of the Antioch College, he made an unsettling discovery. With startling honesty, he summarised the experience as follows:

> "I believed, for example, that a leader could operate successfully as a kind of adviser to his organization. I thought I could avoid being a 'boss'... I thought that maybe I could operate so that everyone would like me –that 'good human relations' would eliminate all discord and disagreement. I couldn't have been more wrong. It took a couple of years, but I finally began to realize that a leader cannot avoid the exercise of authority any more than he can avoid the responsibility for what happens to his organization."[85]

This is the key, of course: there is no authority without responsibility –and vice versa. The individual entrepreneur is characteristically autocratic (often too much, as we saw in Henry Ford's case) because there is so little he can do to avoid the consequences of his actions. This is why, for all the futuristic glamour of their public images, men like Bill Gates of Microsoft, Larry Ellison of Oracle or Steve Jobs of Apple actually have quite an autocratic reputation within their organisations. For the average executive of a large corporation, conversely, it is quite possible to avoid the *appearance* of responsibility (and therefore the blame when things go wrong) by giving up the *appearance* of authority. As Sennett [86] pointedly describes the resulting environment, "power is present [...] but authority is absent." Without authority, there is no ownership of the results –and what no one owns, no one is really concerned about.

For there is a fundamental contradiction in combining avoidance of confrontation with a "coaching" role. The best sport coaches, like the best teachers, do not hesitate to express straightforward feedback to their pupils in order to boost their performance. As a result, of course, they are just as responsible for the success or failure of their trainees as the trainees themselves –in other words, coaching is a way of leading only as long as it involves responsibility. This is why the best coaches often seem to be also the most anxious about the result when their trainees are finally tested: because at the time of the competition there is nothing they can do to help anymore –yet they are still responsible for the result, whatever it is. Exactly the same is the case of the conductor of an orchestra (another widely abused metaphor of the manager's role): his role during the rehearsals is very much like that of a teacher or a couch, but he is still fully responsible for meeting the public's expectations during the performance. Thus, the manager that claims to act only as a couch for his subordinates and uses this statement as an excuse to deflect responsibility for their performance simply has not concept of what leadership is about. For he who does not share in the responsibility of failure but can still send you to the firing squad if you fail to meet certain ill-defined standards is neither a leader nor a coach –is a political commissar.

Among the things I learned shortly after landing in America was a new word: *bullshit*. It is, indeed, a remarkably multipurpose word. In the British Army, according to Norman Dixon, this expression was commonly used to refer to the absurdities of "spit and polish" discipline. He traced its first usage back to the Australian and New Zealander volunteers of the First World War, who, coming as they did from a more liberal, egalitarian society, deeply resented what they quite correctly saw as the result of their officers' insane obsession with appearances. In our modern business world, however, the word is usually applied to the instruments of corporate manipulation, to management half-lies and blue-sky vision/mission statements. Given the disparity of contexts, one might feel tempted to think that *bullshit* did not mean the same for a British battalion in the trenches of the Great War and for the employees of an American corporation in the 1990s. Yet this would be a mistake. For, in either case, the term *bullshit* describes the attempts by those in positions of power to manipulate appearances in order to retain control –even if it is at the expense of the welfare of the team as a whole.

In truth, *bullshit* has always existed and will always exist, simply because brute force does not constitute a solid base from which to govern any society above the level of complexity of a pack of baboons. Power in human societies, therefore, always needs to rest on a delicate web of unspoken assumptions, compromises and expectations –which is why manipulation of people's perceptions has always been both among the most dangerous and the most fragile of Power's weapons. When Nikolai the hermit handed a piece of raw meat to Ivan the Terrible, he was not accusing him of being cruel – the Tsar knew this and did not try to hide it, for he prided himself of being the instrument of God's wrath upon the Earth. In fact, so anxious was the monarch to press this point that he had organised the *opritchniki*, the members of his personal guard, as a sort of monastic order for which he played the role of Grand Master. No: with his simple gesture, the anchorite was accusing the Tsar of being a liar, for it was not divine revenge but his own what he had come to unleash on the citizens of Pskov –and Ivan feared then the Lord's punishment because he knew only too well how far he was from following His command.

Our affluent, democratic, post-modern societies are generally much more reluctant to resort to brute force than any Tsar ever was, and hence power structures need to rely all the more on their ability to manipulate the truth. This is why *bullshit* seems to be everywhere in spades. We see it in national politics, in mass media and, of course, also in business. It is, to some extent, a monument to the progress of equality among human beings that power has to rely less on direct coercion and more to gentle persuasion –even if it is at the cost of distorting the truth. Yet its conspicuous ubiquity, particularly at many large organisations, also bears witness of the intensity of the political struggles that are taking place behind the scenes. Widespread *bullshit* and flight from responsibility in corporate interactions are sure signs that a firm has fallen deep into the pit of office politics, usually as a consequence of an increase in its exposure to uncertainty. Widespread *bullshit* and flight from responsibility in the wider domain of social interactions suggests that it is the wider body social that has been pushed into internal conflict by its failure to adapt quickly enough to an environment of intensified competition. In both cases, these behaviours are aimed at preserving the old structures of power against the markets' unforgiving pressure –and in both cases, unless the increased uncertainty is reversed, they are ultimately as doomed as General Percival's hopes that the danger of a Japanese invasion of Singapore could be made disappear simply by not acknowledging it.

# 9.   HIERARCHIES AND CASH REWARDS

> *"In these complicated times [...] Cash Payment is the sole nexus between man and man."*
>
> - Thomas Carlyle, *Chartism*

One of the few common patterns in pay package structures across countries and historical environments is the premium compensation of the role of bank cashier. At first glance, one would think this an oddity. After all, the job of the cashier of a bank requires neither higher qualifications nor longer working hours than those of the other administration personnel employed at the same branch –yet it consistently yields a higher salary. It has always been done so, and banks, so cost-conscious in many other aspects, do not seem to have ever minded this extra expense. If we ask the bank managers themselves, they will say that the position of cashier is better paid because it carries more "responsibility" –yet it is a responsibility that does not entail any additional decision power. On the face of this, one is forced to conclude that either all the bankers in the world are blind to an obvious cost-reduction opportunity or they actually do reap a material benefit from their generosity towards their cashiers.

The answer is, of course, the latter. What makes the cashier different from the other administrative resources in a bank is that he has direct, daily access to the cash in the safe box, and it would therefore be relatively easy for him to divert some of those funds to his own pocket without being caught. To be sure, the law prescribes fairly harsh punishments for embezzlement, but for the punishment to be meted the crime needs to be proven beyond any reasonable doubt –which usually involves a slow and expensive process with an uncertain outcome that, in any event, very rarely leads to the devolution of the stolen money. Hence, if the bank suspects a cashier is taking advantage of his position to complement his income in this fashion, the logical course of action will in most cases not be to call the police but simply to separate the cashier from his role and fire him. Yet if the cashier were paid no more than the market value of the time and effort he invests in the job, after his sacking he would simply take a similar job elsewhere –and therefore the threat of dismissal would have no bite. It thus makes sense for the bank to pay the cashier a salary above the market clearing wage for his services so that he has a reason to fear losing his job –in other words, to turn the cashier's role into a position of privilege.

Being "privileged" means, in economic terms, to perceive rents above the market value of the services one provides –the specific form under which this "extra" reward takes place being, of course, dependent on the particular structure of the organisation. As in the case of the bank's cashier, a company will be more willing to endow a position with economic privileges the more "responsibility" (defined as ability to shirk without being caught) it carries. From this, of course, follows that precisely the positions in an organisation whose performance is the most difficult to monitor (e.g., those placed higher up in the pecking order) will be the ones privileged with wages higher above the market value of the same level of effort and professional qualification[87]. From the shareholders' viewpoint, these "above-market" rents represent the cost of delegating decision and supervision tasks on an "agent" –i.e., in economic jargon, "agency costs".

This is important because it allows us to measure the way power is allocated across an organisation: the higher the rents a given role is rewarded with, the higher we should conclude is the power associated to it. In a nomadic tribe in the Sahara, a man's power may be measured by the number of sheep, camels and wives he owns. In the European Middle Ages, princes gauged each other's power by looking at the extension of their lands and the number of vassals they could send to war at any given time. But, in our modern capitalist society, cash is king. Hierarchy diagrams can help to some extent to assess who holds power in an organisation, to be sure, but they can also be extremely misleading. A man at the apex of a 10-level corporate hierarchy is not necessarily any more powerful than one on top of only 5 management layers: we already saw how Henry Ford Sr. and his sidekick Harry Bennett held a tyrannical grip on the Ford Motor Co. precisely by reducing the layers of management to the bare minimum. Nor is the man at the apex of the pyramid always the most powerful: anyone familiar with the power dynamics of any hospital where top surgeons make more money than the hospital's director will agree that power is better measured in terms of cash rewards than on the basis of an organisation chart.

This provides us with the tools to dispel a very common myth: that a flatter hierarchy necessarily implies a more even distribution of power. The fact that, throughout the last three decades, corporate hierarchies have effectively flattened has been frequently interpreted by analysts and managers alike as proof that they have become more egalitarian. The evidence that a general corporate "delayering" has indeed taken place is rock-solid, particularly in the USA. For example, a research paper by Raghuram Rajan and Julia Wulf [88] found that the median number of managers reporting to the CEO increased from 4 in 1986 to 7 in 1999 (i.e., by a staggering 75% in barely fourteen years) and that, in general, "the depth, which is the number of positions between the CEO and the lowest managers with profit centre responsibility (division heads), has decreased by more than 25% over the period." These observations become particularly striking if we consider that six or seven is the number of direct reports that most authors (not to talk about every manager's personal experience) regard as the maximum that an executive can effectively manage[89] –yet, if the sample median is seven, it means that 50% of the companies in the survey are already above this maximum. This increase in the average CEO's span of control cannot even be attributed to any unexpected surge in staff numbers that would have caught these organisations' structures out of step: quite on the contrary, the average number of employees of the U.S. corporations in this study went down nearly a 20% throughout those fourteen years. In other words: there must be something very powerful indeed that drives executives to push their span of control even against the natural limits of managerial effectiveness. But what is it?

One might be tempted to conclude that this is due to these organisations having become less hierarchical and more egalitarian – but this would frontally contradict the evidence that derives from people's compensation. For, as we already mentioned in Chapter 1, pay differences have widened to spectacular levels over the same period of time: the average S&P 500 CEO made 30 times more than the average production worker in 1970, but nearly 500 times today. Organisation charts are a bit like the façade of a building: they may or may not reveal what the structure that holds the building together is really like. To understand what is really happening behind the scenes, we need to go back to what we already know about power structures and human nature.

In other words, we need to look back at Figure 4 in Chapter 7 (reproduced again in Figure 5). A highly integrated organisation in a low-risk environment (i.e. an organisation at point A) will pigeon-hole every individual into a given role and a given career path, trying to avoid, to the extent possible, any form of internal conflict. The need to avoid confrontation also means that, if the system is to remain stable, real power will need to be spread throughout the whole hierarchy: for example, when the higher levels enjoy higher pay and other privileges, but the lower ones can expect a job for life, a salary above market-clearing level and the protection of a trade union. This was the landscape at most of the large American corporations in the 1950s, or at the Japanese ones in the 1980s. Even an autocrat like Henry Ford Sr. understood the need to share a piece of the pie in a highly integrated enterprise by paying his workers much more than the competition and providing them with the best social benefits in Detroit. Indeed, it is significant that his (famously bloody) confrontations with the trade unions only really started when, as the company fell behind its competitors throughout the 1930s, its pay and welfare system also became comparatively far less generous than it once had been.

**Figure 5**

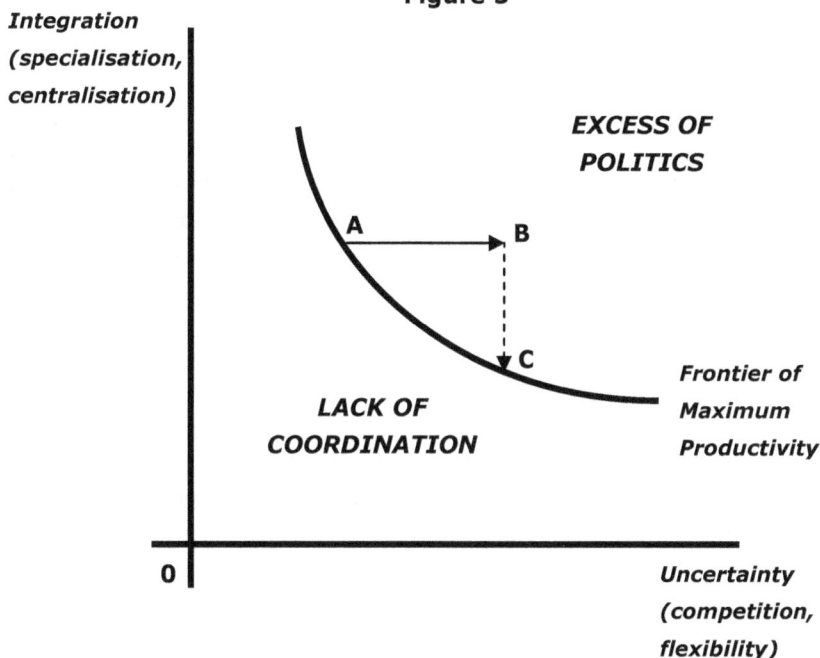

But now imagine that competition intensifies and the business environment shifts the firm from point A to point B in Figure 4. Now, regardless of whether the organisation is able to quickly move down from B to C or resists the challenge and lingers uncomfortably on B, its world will become more of a winner-take-all game. The distance between winners and losers will thus inevitably widen. Yet there is a fundamental difference between being at B and being at C. At point C, the system is composed of a multitude of small teams, maybe separate firms, that are relatively independent of each other, and every one of which can still internally be a tightly-knit group of individuals that know they will float or drown together: the players' fortunes will vary primarily because the most competitive teams will soar while the rest fall.

This does not mean that the governance of each one of these smaller units will necessarily be highly participatory or "democratic". True, in knowledge-intensive industries this tends to be the case, as in the Silicon Valley start-ups of the 1980s or the dot.coms of the 1990s –and these companies are well known for the extraordinary commitment and enthusiasm demonstrated by their members, at least in the initial, "heroic" phase of the business. In other industries where individual creativity is less of a success factor than unity of command, however, the leader's rule can be as absolute as that of the captain of a ship –and for exactly the same reasons. This is how most small family-owned firms are run. In this type of organisation, the tightness of the team is preserved thanks to its paternalistic ways. Thus, the employees of these organisations may be frequently shouted at, but rarely fired. Their salaries may be comparatively low, but they can often ask for a loan with no interests, no set due date and no guarantee other than their goodwill. Their average working hours may be long, but they can often ask for any amount of time off for personal reasons without necessarily using up their vacation allowance. Thus, the paternalism of these firms is aimed at conferring to the organisation the qualities of unity and resilience of a traditional family.

Conversely, at point B the many players are still all closely interdependent (usually as part of the same firm, although the picture does not change much if they have, say, an interdependent customer-vendor relationship). Market pressure is all the same, the competitive game is just as much of a winner-take-all as at point C, but now the conflict takes place primarily within the organisation – which is why it leads to intense politics instead of a true increase in productivity. Within such a company, the winners in this highly complex political game will thus accumulate ever more power at the expense of the losers –and the most visible consequence of this will of course be the concentration of income in fewer hands.

What all this suggests is that, although the last thirty years have seen some significant advances towards point C, the pressure of global competition has grown much faster than large companies could possibly adapt to, and this has left many of them uncomfortably stranded. As a consequence, sure enough, the strength of many of the old power lobbies has been broken: the bargaining power of trade unions has decreased significantly in most developed countries, and middle-management ranks have suffered an even more severe beating. Yet, while this has partially resulted in a long-overdue process of decentralisation, it has also led to a very significant degree of power concentration. As the winner of today's contest knows that there is also a significant risk of losing tomorrow's, it is also rational for him to entrench himself in his privileged position by subdividing the areas of responsibility (read: of power) of his subordinates so that it is not easy for any of them to take his place.

We already saw how this mechanism worked in the case of Marks & Spencer: by refusing to designate a clear *dauphin*, the chairman effectively induced the board to extend his mandate. This is by no means uncommon: the evidence suggests, for example, that CEO's survival rate is significantly higher in companies where no COO (Chief Operations Officer) or CAO (Chief Administration Officer) reports to the CEO[90], or where the responsibilities of chairman of the board and CEO are vested on the same individual[91]. There is a very straightforward logic in this: it is easier to replace a non-performing CEO when there is someone else, a COO for example, playing a shadowing role that covers nearly all of his scope of responsibilities. Under these conditions, a smart CEO will logically apply a divide-and-conquer strategy, subdividing the responsibilities of his subordinates so that no single one of them has visibility to the whole of his tasks.

As the same principle extends down the hierarchy, every executive will try to make his role more irreplaceable by increasing the number of direct reports. This also explains why there seems to be no correlation, once we control for other factors, between the flatness of the organisation chart and the efficiency of the firm[92]. If, as many authors have suggested, flatter hierarchies were spreading because of their being better adapted to modern information technology or to modern management methods, then we would expect flatter hierarchies also to correlate with higher efficiency –but this is just not the case. The data, conversely, reveal a direct correlation between the number of reports to the CEO and the steepness of pay differences between him and the divisional managers[93] –which is exactly what one would expect if the increase in the CEO's control span were due to his entrenchment, i.e., to a process of concentration of power.

To be sure, this concentration of the levers of power in fewer hands will frequently result in inefficient leadership. More than ever, an executive seems to be a man constantly rushing from one meeting to the next while attending a conference call on his mobile phone. Even if we assume, just for the sake of argument, that the time of this individual is not fruitlessly consumed in the endless politics required to stay at a privileged role in these our uncertain times, there is no doubt that overwork is the father of incompetence. This is why wide pay differentials can be a good indicator of managerial inefficiency.

This is by no means a novel observation. In *The Practice of Management*, Peter Drucker quoted, as additional support for his own observations, a research paper published in 1954 and according to which:

> "If the top executive of a company gets a salary seven times as large as the salaries paid to the Number Two, Three and Four men, you can be pretty sure that firm is badly managed. But if the salary levels of the four or five men at the head of the ladder are all close together, then the performance and morale of the entire management group is likely to be high."

> "The size of the salaries doesn't seem to make much difference" the report continued "Whether the president of the corporation gets $20,000 a year or $100,000 isn't important so long as his vice-presidents get something like 70 to 90 percent as much. But when the president pulls down $100,000 and his main subordinates get only $50,000 to $20,000, it is time to look for trouble."[94]

Today, half a century afterwards, these conclusions are still fully consistent with the results of contemporary studies and, while not all scholars agree in their interpretation of this phenomenon, most of them recognise the existence of a significant, positive correlation between wage compression and firm performance [95] . Only, compensation differentials within firms are now much wider than when Drucker wrote his book –and expanding. True, the higher incomes in a company are less secure than they used to be, for the executives who earn them are more likely to be fired if they do not perform, so in a way they are worth less in present value terms –but then again, incomes at the lowest levels have also become less predictable so, on balance, the proportional difference is still much larger than it was.

Of course, it would be tempting to dismiss the impact of large compensation packages as immaterial in the context of the overall economic activity; but this interpretation, once again, would not stand a dispassionate reality check. A recent paper by Lucian Bebchuck & Yanik Grinstein[96], based on a dataset of publicly-traded companies representing more than 80% of the U.S. market capitalisation, concluded that the ratio of the aggregate compensation of the top five individuals in a firm divided by the total net earnings of the firm climbed from an average of 5% in 1993-1995 to about 10% in 2001-2003 (having peaked at nearly 13% in 2000-2002, right before the stock market bubble burst). These are very significant slices of the total value added generated by a firm – all the more significant because the total percentage of national income represented by labour compensation has remained roughly constant (around 70% in the USA) at least since the end of World War II. Approximate as all these aggregate figures undoubtedly are, the implications are inescapable. If the overall participation of labour in the output has not changed, but that of the best paid workers has at least doubled in less than ten years, it means that, on average, everyone else's slice has become smaller. The hierarchical pyramid may have become flatter, but this has only partially translated into decentralisation. To a large extent, the shift into a more uncertain world has led hierarchical power, as evidenced by its underlying cash nexus, to become concentrated into fewer hands. A necessary, perhaps even unavoidable evil this may well be –yet it is an evil nonetheless.

# 10.  TAKING THE PULSE OF THE BUSINESS

*"Competition for power nearly always turns into conflict. [...] The strategy for resolving conflict must be related to the disease, not the symptom. Diagnosis, therefore, differentiating between symptoms and cause, is the key to the proper management of conflict."*

- Charles Handy, *Understanding Organizations*

The most difficult, and at the same time the most critical stage of treating an alcoholic is getting him to accept the very fact of his condition. Especially when the patient is still able to lead a normal, even successful life, piercing the barrier of his obstinate denial is always an arduous and sometimes nearly impossible task. Gentle persuasion is bound to fail under these circumstances, except perhaps to drive home some minor, all-but-cosmetic changes. Brute force might obviously be more effective, but it rarely constitutes a real possibility when dealing with emancipated, self-sustaining adults. Often, therefore, the only glimmer of hope rests on the therapist's ability to confront the subject with crisp, measurable, undeniable evidence.

Corporate denial is, if anything, even more difficult to tackle. We have already seen how the intricate web of vested interests that permeates an organisation conspires to turn its members, and particularly its leadership, into its worst enemies. As long as the business is still successful, denial will usually persist unashamedly until reality strikes under the form of a failure too painful to ignore – but by this time it may be way too late. This is what happened to Enron, to WorldCom, to Marks & Spencer... Despite the warning signals, all these organisations seemed to be steaming full speed ahead when catastrophe struck them dead on their tracks. Of course, if the investors had realised that this was going to happen, the market ratings of these firms would have taken a beating, and this in itself could have acted as an early warning signal –but they did not. In each one of these cases, the external evidence of deterioration of these businesses' long-term prospects was too weak and subjective to counterweight the hard, measurable fact of their growing quarterly returns.

For, indeed, how could one spot when an organisation is mired in an excess of office politics? Charles Handy[97], on the basis of quite an impressive array of previous literature, enumerates the following six main symptoms of organisational conflict:

1.  Poor communications (or miscommunications) laterally and vertically.

2.  Inter-group hostility and jealousy.

3.  Inter-personal friction.

4.  Frequent escalation of arbitration.

5.  Proliferation of rules and regulations, norms and myths.

6.  Low morale of the type expressed in frustration at inefficiency, mostly directed at the higher levels of the organisation ("you would think they didn't want anything to happen...").

While these points are certainly useful, they are neither present in all organisations suffering from an excess of politics (there is always at least one, but rarely all of them at the same time) nor necessarily absent from all properly-functioning ones. Hence, there is an open question about how much escalation, or how much regulation, for instance, is really too much. This, nevertheless, would still pose a workable challenge if it were not for another, more fundamental issue: there is no reliable way to measure these behavioural patterns, particularly for an external observer. Actually, all organisations go out of their way to discourage, deflect or punish the expression of their internal frustrations to the outside world ("we wash our dirty linen at home"), *especially* when there are good reasons for it. This is why, when disaster strikes, it is often only outsiders (and, funnily enough, top management) who seem to be genuinely surprised.

There is therefore a case for identifying an alternative set of relatively "objective" metrics that can be used to provide some robustness to the diagnostic. Among the many potential indicators, I have listed below the ones that seem to be best supported by the evidence available. Just as in the case of the six "classical" behavioural traits we have listed above, we should not expect them to appear all together in every single troubled organisation, nor to manifest themselves solely in dysfunctional corporations. Yet their consistent presence at many organisations known to have had problems related to excessive internal politics strongly suggest that, if two or more of these indicators happen to be found at a particular business, there is a reasonable case to expect it to suffer from this type of disease as well.

Before we proceed, however, a cautionary point should be made. What fundamentally characterises a company suffering from an "excess of politics" is that it is too short-term focused for its integrated processes to work efficiently —or, what is the same, it depends too heavily on an internal cooperation that it does not stimulate enough. Thus, simply measuring the firm's cost of capital (which would provide an indication of the rate at which its leadership team discounts the foreseeable future outcome of its decisions) would not necessarily tell us much: a high discount rate might just be fine for a company with a decentralised structure, while a lower one could have a poisonous effect on a more integrated enterprise. Comparing with other firms within the same industry may be a bit more interesting but, to the extent a whole industry can be thrown into excess of politics by a change in the prevalent market conditions, this might not always raise the appropriate alarm signals. Therefore, although the cost of capital should always be considered, it does not, all by itself, constitute solid evidence of a damaging short-term bias unless it is associated to other tell-tale signs like the one listed below:

## 1. High level of financial leverage:

This is perhaps the variable whose link to corporate short-term thinking is most reliably supported by empirical evidence[98]. When things do not go well in a business, one of the most conspicuous indicators of it is, of course, a decline in the free cash flow it generates. Now, a fall in the free cash flow is not necessarily an indicator of short-term thinking, to be sure. In some cases it may actually constitute an indication of the opposite (e.g., it could be due to increased investment in R&D). Yet when the "hole" is consistently being financed through debt, and in particular through short-term liabilities, this may be a symptom that the company's leaders are using financial leverage (i.e., accumulation of debt) as an "easy way out" of a problem whose solution would require a longer-term approach. Ultimately, aggressive financial gearing entails, other things being equal, an increase in the risk associated to corporate equity and therefore, at least in high-variability industries, it may well indicate an underlying problem for which management is trying to find a quick fix by raising the bets. Research papers indicate[99] that, at least in "high dynamism" industries (i.e., markets under high variability or, what is the same, uncertainty), high levels of financial leverage are statistically correlated to lower performance over the long run. In addition, financial leverage can start a vicious cycle, as the pressure to meet the debt payment terms will increase the short-term pressure on the organisation, which may result in further deterioration of its market positioning, which may eventually lead to a further need for credit to plug a bigger hole, etc.

## 2. Abnormally high or rapidly growing profit-on-sales ratio:

When something seems too good to be true, it usually is. While profit is obviously a good thing, when the profitability growth rate is significantly higher than that of comparable companies in the same industry, one should look for a strong reason why –or else wonder whether there may be an issue of managerial myopia behind the scenes. The rationale is that, if at a certain point in time corporate decisions become more short-term focused, profitability should be expected to go up, at least for a while, because costs whose benefit is only observable in the long run (say, research, customer service or simply the quality of the input materials) can be reduced. We have already seen how this happened in the case of Marks & Spencer, where not only were costs systematically reduced at the expense of service quality, but the price tag of rapid-selling products would often be raised instead of keeping it low to act as a customer reclaim. A similar situation took place at IBM with the S/390 mainframe system in the early 1990s. According to Lou Gerstner, when he took over in 1993 he found out that the market share of Big Blue's flagship product was being gradually eroded because its price was nearly 50% above that of its closest competitors. Yet the reason was not related to production costs: the price was kept deliberately high so that this product's profit could help finance the losses of the rest of the firm –in other words, the long-term asset was being bled for the sake of short-term cash flow[100].

## 3. Abnormally high rate of return on investment:

In financial institutions and related risk-brokerage businesses, the strategy of increasing today's margins at the expense of tomorrow's viability can also take place through the expedient of moving into riskier forms of investment (e.g., lending to companies with a low credit rating), which of course carry a higher yield. In Enron's case, for example, the firm achieved its highest level of profitability precisely in 1998 and 1999, the two years prior to its collapse[101]. By that time, the firm had plunged head-on into its energy trader role and was therefore reaping the immediate benefits of its assumption of higher levels of risk. This is also what happened at some of the most famous scandals in the investment banking business, although the responsibility did not always belong directly to the bank as an institution but to traders (e.g., Nick Leeson at Barings) who would try to cover their losses before they would be noticed by investing in high risk assets. In a way, when a company increases its financial leverage it is implicitly moving into a riskier business model –in other words, there is a very close link between this indicator and the level of financial gearing.

4. **Low levels of customer and/or employee satisfaction:**

Perhaps the most intuitively self-evident indicator of all, this one tries to identify the sources of trouble in people's perceptions. If cost cuts have been made at the expense of product quality or customer service, or have had an impact on the level of staff motivation, measures like these may be able to raise an alert signal before it is too late. As we have already seen, one of the most conspicuous early warning signals in the case of Marks & Spencer was a decline in both customer and employee satisfaction that was traceable on anecdotal evidence at least as far back as 1995 or 1996. A similar comment could be made about IBM during its struggling years. Interestingly, although empirical studies tend to confirm the positive correlation between customer satisfaction and business results, the relationship has been found not to be very strong[102]. This, however, should not really be a surprise, for the intuitive relationship is between customer and employee satisfaction and *long-term* performance, whereas in the short run a company can sacrifice the satisfaction of these key stakeholders for the sake of short-term profitability. In other words, in the short run the relationship between profitability and stakeholder satisfaction goes in reverse. In any event, the evidence also suggests that the opposite implication cannot be made (i.e., if everyone is happy, then everything must be all right): indeed, the levels of customer and employee satisfaction at some of the most notorious corporate failures of recent times (e.g., Enron or Adelphia) were remarkably high.

## 5. Reduced level of investment in long-term-relevant items:

This one is fairly obvious, yet surprisingly frequent. An example taken from my own experience may help to illustrate how this can happen. A large producer of clinical diagnostics devices found at a certain point that it was losing ground fast to its main competitors. A preliminary analysis revealed that the problem was that the research department had too long a development cycle, in a market where being able to launch the most sophisticated devices before the competition is what grants the highest product margins. As a consequence, a cross-functional team was set up with great fanfare and charged with the task of finding out the root causes of the poor performance of the laboratories. Yet the answer was readily available, and it was the CFO who volunteered it to us without even asking: for the previous five years, every time it seemed that the net profit was not going to reach its targets, the first expenditure item that would be cut back was Research and Development –no wonder R&D was taking long to develop its products!

## 6. Complex cost-and-revenue allocation rules:

Let's face it: accounting does not need to be terribly complicated. At many companies, however, it seems to be an obscure art, particularly as it refers to attribution of costs.

EDUARD GRACIA

In highly political organisations, cost and revenue allocations become a political weapon, and the result is that their rules can become extremely (and unnecessarily) complex. For example, a large chemical group allocated out all the costs generated at the headquarters down to every product and every subsidiary –even the costs of a Japanese garden they had at the headquarters' building were allocated this way. This was of course a way for the head office to avoid being subject to scrutiny regarding those costs, but at the same time turned the concept of cost of goods sold into a useless magnitude. Under these conditions, a product line could be selling at a loss, from a controlling viewpoint, because, although every single unit sold might well have a positive contribution to the bottom line, the allocated costs from the headquarters (which did not depend on the units sold) exceed the marginal profit. Needless to say, the result was endless discussion and political peddling around the allocation rules. It should be clear to us at this point, however, that the real issue was not so much the cost allocation technology as the excessive centralisation of a hierarchical whose business was driven by more local factors. This allowed the headquarters to dump costs on their subsidiaries while still holding them responsible for their accounting results.

## 7. Long, cumbersome planning and budgeting cycle:

It is easy to see why this is a good indicator of excess of politics. In a decentralised organisation working in an uncertain market, planning will logically take place primarily bottom-up, under the form of a performance contract where each profit centre manager separately agrees to a set of targets that is considers realistic. Conversely, in a centralised firm operating in a highly predictable environment, planning will primarily be decided top-down as a mandate issued by the centre to the subsidiaries, and therefore the centre alone will be responsible for making sure it is realistic. In an organisation that is too centralised for the level of uncertainty it is subject to, however, the top brass will try to use their power to impose aggressive targets down the hierarchy but at the same time expect the profit centre managers to take ownership for them. In turn, the profit centre managers will obviously pushback but, since the organisation is too hierarchical for them to dare openly expressing their resistance, they have no choice but to drag their feet and renegotiate behind the scenes. Thus, the planning and budgeting cycle becomes a long, extremely complicated bargaining exercise where many of the key decisions seem to be made in smoke-filled rooms after endless iterations of the same number-crunching exercise. Planning thus turns into a dangerous political game where every manager tries to buy easy targets for himself and wholly unrealistic ones for his rivals

This problem has actually become so serious and widespread in the last decades that it has prompted some authors to put forward a set of radical remedies. For instance, in their book *Beyond Budgeting*, Robin Fraser and Jeremy Hope go so far as to propose doing away with the traditional budgeting process altogether[103]. Their recipe is in fact fairly consistent with the reasoning we have followed here: by moving away from a rigid budgeting cycle and towards a more flexible set of periodic forecasting exercises, they effectively turn the process into a more bottom-up, less centralised mechanism. To the extent most companies are suffering today from an excess of politics due to their excessive centralisation, therefore, this can only be a good thing. Yet, as Fraser and Hope themselves acknowledge, and as we have consistently highlighted throughout this book, any effort in this direction should expect to face significant resistance to change –for the privileges granted by centralisation never go away without a fight.

8. **Wide compensation gap from one hierarchy level to the next:**

We have already devoted the whole of Chapter 9 to explain how this may signal an issue, so there would be no point in repeating the argument now. Suffice it to say that, of all the indicators we have seen here, this is probably the most neglected. It is a well-known sociological fact that the most internally cooperative teams are those where the members feel the most over-privileged respective to outsiders and the least under-privileged respective to each other. From the viewpoint of the ideas put forward in this book, this simply means that there is a maximum incentive to work to keep the overall team successful, and a minimum incentive to intrigue to obtain the next promotion. Military history, once again, provides some striking examples. For instance, the most disciplined and effective soldiers of the Renaissance, the mercenaries in the Swiss infantry, were also by far the most egalitarian (the Swiss Confederation being quite literally the only democratic country of that era). Their "secret" was that, precisely because of their sharing the dangers as well as the profit of their profession in a similar measure, every one of them was willing to police that everyone else would do his duty. Our modern corporations may be set for a less murderous intent, but human nature still remains the same.

Then again, none of these indicators in isolation would constitute absolute evidence of the existence of an issue. One could, for example, imagine the case of a company in serious difficulty that hired an external, highly expensive leadership team that then issued debt to raise cash in order to perform well-overdue investments and cut costs through the implementation of new technology. In this example, if we measured most of these indicators at the time the new team had just started to work and not yet managed to change the negative perception of customers and employees inherited from the previous situation, the firm would obviously score quite poorly –

despite its being on the path of recovery. Yet, for the most part, this "false alarm" would simply be the confirmation that things always get worse before they get better. Like the patient that submits to surgery, or the drug addict that endures a "cold turkey" detox treatment, the company that is on the path to recovery often looks worse than before for a while –yet the same symptoms in an individual, or a firm, that is not undergoing treatment ought to be regarded as a strong indication that something may not be quite right.

# AFTERWORD: THE ROAD AHEAD

> *"Today's world economy is inherently less stable and more anarchic than the liberal international economic order which collapsed in 1914. [...] If we take history as our guide, we must expect that the global free market will shortly belong to an irrecoverable past."*

> - John Gray, *False Dawn: The Delusions of Global Capitalism*

We are about to reach the end of this book's journey. We have talked about what factors can intensify office politics in an organisation, and how this can be a consequence of external market circumstances as much as of internal ones. We have explained why many large organisations now seem to suffer more from internal politics and widespread *bullshit* than ever, and what role liberalisation and globalisation have played in this drama. There is one logical next question left, though, and I would not like to conclude without devoting a few final words to it: *where do we go from here?* The answer can only be highly speculative, to be sure, but then again every planning exercise relies on such speculation, and good planning is the cornerstone of competent management. After all, beyond the walls of the corporate office there is a wider human society whose rules determine how and under what conditions business can (or cannot) be conducted. The question of where the overall business environment may go throughout the next few decades is therefore relevant enough for us to risk gazing into the crystal ball.

The pendulum of History has already swung back and forth many times between intervention and liberalisation. In a doubtlessly oversimplified generalisation, we could say that the European societies of the *Ancien Régime* were eminently static and conservative. Social mobility was arrested by laws that assigned to each and every one a specific place in society purely on the grounds of birth right. Manufacturing was regulated by guilds, and commerce was severely limited by the feudal lords' right to impose arbitrary taxation. In the 18th Century, most European countries followed a "mercantilist" (i.e., protectionist) foreign policy, using import tariffs and state monopolies to impose controls on the economic activity. In the first years of the 19th Century, Napoleon tried to transform Continental Europe into a huge protectionist fortress stretching from Portugal to Russia, in a vain attempt to choke the economy of Great Britain, which was already in the full heat of industrialisation. This was to be the high tide of mercantilism in Europe for nearly a hundred years: after Napoleon's defeat, and until the 1870s, Britain's pressure would gradually lead to a general reduction of tariff barriers. Democracy and liberalism spread over the globe. Slavery, that millennial scourge of mankind, was abolished nearly everywhere. Economic growth and technological progress reached absolutely unprecedented levels. Then, as we saw in Chapter 6, around 1870 the pendulum started to swing again towards interventionism. Slowly at first, but then increasingly faster after the First World War and the Great Depression of 1929, international trade waned, and totalitarian regimes spread like a malignant cancer. By 1940, one could have counted the number of democratic regimes still remaining in Europe with the fingers in one hand. This was another high tide of interventionism –and much higher than the previous one it was. Then, as we saw in Chapter 7, after the end of World War II the system began to globalise again, in a process that has essentially continued until today.

Overall, it is probably accurate to state that today's world economy is the most globally interdependent ever (albeit not necessarily, it must be said, the most liberal[104]). The Soviet Block dissolved a mere fifteen years ago, and the economies of India, Indonesia or China are liberalising at increasing speed. Technology has made physical distance almost literally irrelevant from a business perspective, perhaps most spectacularly through the internet. As a consequence, numerous services which not so long ago could only be delivered by local workers are now being routinely transferred ("off-shored") to cheap-labour locations in East Asia, Eastern Europe or Latin America. Meanwhile, the European Union has grown to 25 countries representing most of the population and the economic power of the continent. These countries have removed, or are in the process of removing, nearly all formal trade barriers against each other, and most of them now even share a single currency –the Euro. A similar (though far less wide-ranging) development has taken place in the Americas through the NAFTA agreements. At the same time, intense migratory movements from poorer countries are contributing to fill in the generation cohort gaps that the low birth rate of the most developed nations had left throughout the last few decades. Related to these phenomena are the growth of the variable component of pay packages (whose most visible form are probably stock options) and the pressures for large businesses to decentralise (e.g., through outsourcing of non-core components of the business or through the creation of joint ventures and spin-off initiatives). Indeed, when historians looks back at our times, they may well regard the peak of the dot.com boom as a high water mark of the long globalisation wave that took off with the end of World War II.

Yet with the economic crisis that followed the dot.com era came increasing pushback. The most visible aspect of this, albeit probably also the one with the smallest impact, is the growing anti-globalisation movement, whose most spectacular achievement so far has been the collapse in 2003 of the World Trade Organisation conferences in Cancún, Mexico. Behind this movement, however, there is a sense of increasing unrest amid significant portions of the population of the developed world, which results in political pressure to stop and even reverse globalisation. No wonder: in the context of global competition against cheap-labour offshore locations, the privileges represented by social protection rules in developed countries are obviously in jeopardy. As a matter of fact, it is not only the price impact of these cheap competitors but also, and maybe most unsettlingly for those impacted, the increased share of the overall business risk that now rests on the shoulders of the average workers in a developed country. Not only does the variable portion of their salary constitute a larger proportion of the whole, not only does the law provide them with less protection against layoffs than it used to, but even retirement pensions are now increasingly dependent on the uncertainties of the financial markets' performance, as opposed to being tied only to past salary levels and contributions.

The limits imposed since the 1980s on the scope of protection provided by the welfare state in most Western societies should probably be credited with a significant contribution to the global economic growth we all witnessed in the 1990s. In any event, as long as most people were to a greater or lesser extent riding the growth wave, few found any real reason to complain. Yet as the downside of risk shows again its ugly head, we should expect discontent to set in among those who feel the pain –and we should expect them to use their political muscle to express it. It was, after all, the Great Depression of 1873-1879 (which, incidentally, started as a financial crash following a global railway investment boom, just as the 2001 stock market crash followed a period of overinvestment in technology stocks) that triggered the backlash against globalisation in the 19th Century. History has a discomforting tendency to repeat itself.

Government intervention is now expanding again in many areas. In the wake of the financial scandals that hit the news in rapid succession at the start of the 21st Century, many countries raised the bar of their legal requirements for corporate governance. This includes rules like the Sarbanes-Oxley Act for companies subject to the U.S. Stock Exchange Commission (SEC), the Operational and Financial Reporting (OFR) requirements for firms quoted on the London Stock Exchange, the Basel II Agreements for financial institutions, etc. Anti-money-laundering measures against terrorism and drug-traffic, despite their avowed non-economic purposes, have similarly resulted in tighter controls. In order to comply with these legal requirements for additional external reporting and internal controls, corporations will have no choice but to become more bureaucratic. Yet, highly visible as all this is, it is but one aspect of a general shift.

Another one is the increasing pressure towards rebuilding trade barriers between the different trade blocks. Trade negotiations between the USA and the European Union, or between either of these and China, have become particularly hard in the last few years. Accusations of American unilateralism have become a lot louder and, at least in some instances, a lot better grounded. The E.U. is experiencing mounting pressure to limit or slow down its extension to new countries (note, for instance, the widespread opposition to the start of entry negotiations with Turkey). Meanwhile, the U.S. Government is experiencing similar pressures against the signature of a Central America Free Trade Agreement (CAFTA) that would in effect extend NAFTA to the countries between Mexico and Colombia. Partially (but, it must be said, only partially) in order to increase protection against terrorism, immigration rules are becoming a lot tougher on both sides of the Atlantic. Even currency areas are now under attack. The number of economies whose currency is pegged to the U.S. Dollar has been steadily declining since the Asian crash in 1998. Argentina's is probably the most spectacular case, but China's recent decision to loosen its peg (interestingly enough, under strong U.S. pressure to do so) may well prove to be the most momentous in the long run. Most intriguingly of all, the Italian government has recently even put forward a proposal to call a referendum in order to decide whether the country should stay in the Eurozone or return to its own national currency. Even if, as all evidence suggests, this is no more than a misled public relations manoeuvre that is bound to lead nowhere, it is certainly representative of a widespread mood.

So we are at a crossroad. This backlash may turn up to be a mere blip in the context of the secular march towards global economic liberalization, or it may turn up to be the beginning of a swing back to interventionism. To a large extent, whether we end up going in one direction or the other will depend on what happens in the next few years. If the current trend towards economic recovery proves resilient enough and we return to something similar to the growth patterns of the 1990s, then all is well for further liberalisation. Yet if not –and there are a number of reasonable alternative scenarios that might halt this trend– then we may witness how the pendulum swings back against economic liberalism. If, for example (and this is squarely in the realm of speculation, to be sure) there were another serious dip in the value of the assets that most people in developed countries rely on to finance their retirements (be it stock market valuations or, even worse, real state prices), we should expect to see mounting political pressure for governments to step in to fill the gap. Or, if the now-booming economy of China collapsed just the same way Brazil's did in the 1980s (and the similarities between the two are startling, including the widespread corruption that ultimately turned Brazil's economic miracle into a financial catastrophe), then other governments might be compelled to raise their trade barriers to prevent contagion –just as they did in the 1930s when the U.S. economy collapsed. I am not saying that any of these gloomy scenarios is necessarily bound to happen, of course –but the probability is not insignificant, and they should by no means be ignored.

*****

What does this all mean from a corporate strategy viewpoint? The consequences of the recent backlash against liberalisation can already be seen. For example, enthusiasm for outsourcing seems to be on the wane. Companies increasingly see less of an advantage in relying on external providers for many of their business processes, as they start to see some outsourcing contracts as the equivalent of throwing themselves in the clutches of a monopolist. There is still, conversely, a significant advantage in placing shared service facilities at low-cost offshore locations, as long as the company still retains control. This, in short, suggests that large corporations will be more capable of taking advantage of these synergies that smaller ones. Economies of scale and scope may now be back at the top of the strategist's toolkit.

At the same time, there is also an increased emphasis on tighter, more rigorous (shall we say "Taylorist"?) methodologies. The shift is probably most visible in the market of Information Technology, particularly as it relates to software development and deployment work. Not so long ago, software development was the archetypical domain of creative mavericks for whom the discipline of a methodology was as helpful as a bag of sand in the gas tank of a car. Over time, methodologies were developed and used, to be sure, but the most successful ones always allowed enough freedom for the experts to use their creativity –one could have said they acted more as checklists than as sets of prescriptions. Interestingly, the dynamics of the IT market in the 1980s were often taken by many of the most popular management gurus of the 90s as the model of the organisation of the future. These authors hailed a new world where professionals would routinely work as subcontractors, self-employed temporary workers alternating periods of intense activity with others of transitory unemployment (which they would use to recycle their skills), and who would often not even show up at the office to work, but simply use the web to log in from home. Some even called this – don't laugh now– the "leisure society".

As IT services are increasingly provided from offshore centres operating factory-style, however, they also need to submit to a more rigorous work regime. Thus, IT work is more and more often required to submit to strict methodologies such as the Capability Maturity Model (CMM), which in essence tries to ensure all processes are controlled, documented and repeatable on the basis of their documentation –in other words, that there is a tight level of bureaucratic control. This is by no means an isolated development: today, the processes at most of the large IT support facilities in Hyderabad or Bangalore in India, as well as many of the ones in other countries, are certified at CMM Level 5 –the highest level of CMM compliance certification. In accounting, which is obviously the enterprise function that has been most heavily impacted by the recent financial scandals, Sarbanes-Oxley and Basel II regulation have already forced to an additional bureaucratisation of processes, and the general expectation is that the nearly future will bring more of the same. Nor is this phenomenon constrained to IT or accounting: the surge of interest in production control methodologies such as Six Sigma bears witness of the shift of emphasis in production processes from creativity and flexibility to quality and control.

One could also associate this "re-Taylorisation" of production procedures to the process of concentration we are also witnessing in many industries. The recent wave of mergers and acquisitions on both sides of the Atlantic may well be a temporary phenomenon fuelled by low interest rates and the expectations of economic recovery after the crash, but concentration is a reality in a number of key sectors. The most spectacular example is probably the commercial aircraft industry. After the acquisition of McDonnell-Douglas by Boeing in 1996, this market has become a strict duopoly between the latter and Airbus −each one of the contenders being fiercely backed by the subsidies and other protectionist policies of its corresponding home government or trading block. At a cross-industry level, some authors[105] suggest that, after reaching a trough towards the end of the eighties, the degree of industry concentration has tended to increase, at least in the USA. If governments start to move decisively towards more protectionist measures, we should also expect corporations in other markets to slide towards some form of concentration as well −and tiny yet successful start-ups of the type that became so common in the late 1990s to become increasingly rare.

Just like a physical pendulum, History needs some time to regain momentum after every change of direction. Therefore, we should not be surprised to find that the shifts are relatively small from a historical perspective −after all, the previous interventionist era also started quite harmlessly with a few tariff raises triggered by a global recession. In this context, as in any other climate change, survival will be the reward of the fittest.

Looking at the way this type of shift took place in the past, one can already identify two obvious pitfalls along the way. The first one is the knee-jerk tendency of companies and individuals to respond to new circumstances by doing more of the same. We already saw in Chapter 7, for example, how the first reaction of many corporations to the intensified competition in the late sixties was to embark on a renewed programme of acquisitions to hedge off market risk through economies of scale and scope. These same overextended businesses would barely ten years thereafter become the preferred victims of the takeover sharks of the early 1980s. In the same vein, there is now a risk for many companies to react by demanding even more flexibility, by introducing an even larger variable component in their pay packages, by subdividing themselves into even more internally-competing departments, by cutting down non-contributory benefits... in sum, by transferring even more of their risk to their employees. Like the driver that steps on the brake pedal to stop a car that is sliding out of control on an icy road, such an approach is likely to make things worse, even if it feels better in the short term. If change is due to stronger interventionist winds blowing over the long term, chances are that stories like the one we saw in Chapter 6 about IBM in the 1930s will prove to be the most successful. Scale, scope and an internally stable environment may prove to be critical to corporate success once again.

The second danger is much more insidious, and in many aspects runs opposite to the first. We have already seen how, left to their own devices, organisation hierarchies will always tend to stiffen, to push the productive process to ever higher levels of integration. This is simply because those in whose power it is to define the future course of the organisation are also those who, due to their privileged positions, are the first beneficiaries of centralising ever more power in their hands. In a liberalisation process like the one under whose influence we have been for the last forty years or so, the market effectively acts as a check against these self-serving tendencies. While the conflict that results is never a pretty sight and, by throwing the firms that resist to decentralisation into the deep end of excess of politics, tends to make things worse before they get better, in the end natural selection does its job. Yet interventionism is aimed precisely at weakening this role of the market as a control mechanism, and therefore allows centralisation to flourish.

The 20<sup>th</sup> Century saw how extreme interventionism (otherwise known as "totalitarianism") engendered the twin nightmares of Fascism and Communism. In the absence of the external reference of a free market, the ultra-centralised industrial web of the Soviet Block turned factories into huge value destroying machines, where the market value of the raw materials they used, even without considering labour or cost of capital, was often higher than that of the products they produced. Albeit at a far smaller scale, to be sure, corporations should beware any tendencies to centralisation that are not granted by a robust business case. This danger is already turning into a reality: at many of the firms that have adopted the internal controls required by the Sarbanes-Oxley Act throughout the last two years, one can already see how the interpretation of the legal text is often stretched beyond recognition by the internal bureaucrats (usually, but not exclusively, the internal audit and IT departments) to cover areas that are obviously outside the Act's original intent. As a consequence, additional requirements for approval signatures and quality reviews proliferate, and the inefficiencies that derive from them are presented as the unavoidable cost of legal compliance. This is a very old political power-grabbing trick and, if the general trend towards interventionism continues, one that companies should be extremely wary of. For, it is true, those who do not adapt to the new conditions will not survive –but those who use them as an excuse to impose additional bureaucratic paralysis on their processes will by no means fare any better.

*****

When an alcoholic drinks a glass of liquor after having abstained for a long time, it feels to him like going to Heaven after a long stay in Hell. His sense of relief is real, and for good reason: his body has developed a dependency, and now it feels a lot better with a bit of alcohol in his veins. Sometimes the need is so strong that the side effects of abstinence can become truly dangerous. This, however, constitutes no evidence at all that the liquor will do him any good in the long run –for, even in the best case, it will lengthen his dependency. Economic intervention can have a similar effect on a system that is undergoing a process of liberalisation. We have seen this everywhere throughout this book: when a system that is subject to liberalisation does not decentralise quickly enough, intensified competition leads to conflict and concentration of power. The issues we have highlighted bear witness of the fact that we live in a world in painful transition. Liberalisation and global competition have the potential to breed rapid long-term growth (as they have already demonstrated over the two hundred years since the Industrial Revolution), but only when and to the extent old structures of privilege can be demolished at the same time. Yet, as those who benefit from these structures obviously resist to the market's pressure for change, the cure is inevitably painful. Under these conditions, economic intervention, like a glass of liquor for an alcoholic, has the tantalising appeal of instant relief –even if it leads to worse consequences in the long run. This is why calls for intervention become so much louder in times of economic hardship.

There are many well-known examples of how intervention can ease but also prolong the pain. For example, in the 1970s steelworks and mining in both Western Europe and the USA started to become grossly uncompetitive against their East Asian rivals. In Western Europe (particularly in Continental Europe), the government's reaction was for the most part to support these industries through ever-increasing subsidies and tariff protection. In the USA, conversely, very little government help came forth and, as a consequence, Pittsburgh, once the undisputed world capital of steel production, slid down deep into industrial decadence. Yet, twenty years thereafter, the picture had changed radically. By the 1990s there was not a single steel mill left in Pittsburgh, but the town had turned into a flourishing hub for numerous other businesses like chemicals or high-tech. Conversely, most of the decadent steel towns in Continental Europe that have enjoyed public subsidies and protection for all these decades are still as depressed as ever.

The most compelling counterexample is probably Russia's liberalisation process in the nineties[106]. The Soviet Union was, until the very day of its dissolution, one of the most hierarchical, centralised human organisations conceivable, built on the basis of one of the most inefficient productive systems on Earth. It achieved some degree of balance by providing its citizens with an environment where they were sheltered from most of the uncertainty of a free market system –although it could never be nearly enough to eliminate the chronic excess of politics the system suffered. When in 1991 the system finally collapsed, the Russian government initiated, with the support and encouragement of the IMF and the World Bank, a process of economic liberalisation. Yet, as all the levers of power were still in the hands of the same members of the *nomenklatura* that had held them in the old regime, it was wholly unrealistic to expect them to dismantle these structures of privilege that served them so well. Hence, the Russian economy was suddenly exposed to much more competitive uncertainty than ever before, but this was not accompanied by a significant reduction of the underlying web of privileges. It became a cutthroat, winner-take-all market, in many aspects not unlike America in the wild days of the robber barons and the first crime syndicates. Yet, as the power structures of the soviet days had not disappeared, the result was political conflict, fabulous concentration of wealth in the hands of a few well-connected individuals and, ultimately, inefficiency, corruption and waste as a scale that almost beggars belief. Soon, many people even started to ask for a return to the policies of the soviet era. Nonetheless, I hope after reading this book it will appear as evident to the reader that the problem in Russia was not liberalisation *per se*, but rather its combination with a hierarchical privilege system that, despite the naïve expectations that many expressed in the early nineties, simply refused to just go away.

The frequently critical tone I adopted in some of the chapters of this book when discussing the impact of market liberalisation on corporate dynamics might lead some to think that the opposite would be good news on all fronts. This would be a serious misinterpretation. Reducing the environment's uncertainty through interventionism does initially reduce the pressure for conflict, but at the price of growing and stiffening the maze of privileges that caused the conflict in the first place. This is just as true of corporations as it is of any other type of human organisation. If the regulatory environment becomes more interventionist, the biggest challenge will be for business organisations to remind themselves that it is always easier to move towards integration than the opposite, simply because it is much easier to create hierarchical privileges than to dissolve them. Therefore, if they intend to survive in the long run, they will need to constantly remind themselves, against the deafening pressure of the multiple vested interests that surround them, that any bureaucratic privileges they set up above and beyond what is strictly unavoidable will become a potentially lethal dead weight when global liberalisation eventually resumes its course.

For each and every one of us who try to make a living in this our uncertain world, the most insidious if not the biggest danger is that of failing to distinguish between fact and *bullshit*, between information and manipulation. In the jungle of corporate smoke and mirrors, the power mist that fills offices and meeting rooms is often so dense, the political balances so subtle, the ultimate responsibilities so difficult to pinpoint that it becomes exceedingly hard to see where things really stand. Yet, when this happens, we may still find some personal comfort in remembering that, of all possible sources of power, deception constitutes the most unstable of all. After all, a semi-naked Russian hermit once brought a Tsar to his knees simply by calling him a liar and offering to him a piece of raw meat.

# BIBLIOGRAPHY

Adams, Scott (1996) *The Dilbert Principle* Harper Business.

Atkinson, Anthony; Bourguignon, François & Morrison, C. (1992) *Empirical Studies of Earnings Mobility* Harwood Academic Publishers.

Bauman, Zygmunt (2000) *Liquid Modernity* (reprint, 2003) Blackwell.

Bebchuck, Lucian & Grinstein, Yaniv (2005) "The Growth of Executive Pay" *Harvard John M. Olin Discussion Paper,* 510.

Beck, Ulrich (1992) *Risk Society: Towards a New Modernity* (English translation from German original) Sage.

Berger, Philip G. & Ofek, Eli (1995) "Diversification's Effect on Firm Value" *Journal of Financial Economics* 37(1).

Bevan, Judi. 2001. *The Rise and Fall of Marks & Spencer* Profile Books.

Birkinshaw, Julian (2003) "The Paradox of Corporate Entrepreneurship" *Strategy + Business Magazine,* Spring.

Bodily, Samuel E. & Brunner, Robert F. (2002) "Enron: 1986-2001" *Darden Case No.: UVA-G-0563-M-SSRN.*

Campbell, John Y. & Viceira, Luis M. (2002) *Strategic Asset Allocation* (reprint, 2003) Oxford University Press.

Chandler, Alfred D. (1977) *The Visible Hand: The Managerial Revolution in American Business* (reprint, 2002) Harvard University Press.

Chandler, Alfred D. (1990) *Scale and Scope: The Dynamics of Industrial Capitalism* (reprint, 2004) Harvard University Press.

Comment, Robert & Jarrell, Gregg (1995) "Corporate Focus and Stock Returns" *Journal of Financial Economics* 37(1).

Coase, Ronald H. (1937) "The Nature of the Firm" *Economica 16*, November.

Comanor, William S. & Miyao, Takahiro (1985) "The Organization and Relative Productivity of Japanese and American Industry" *Managerial and Decision Economics* 6.

Dixon, Norman (1976) *On the Psychology of Military Incompetence* Jonathan Cape.

Donkin, Richard (2001) *Blood, Sweat & Tears: The Evolution of Work* Texere.

Drucker, Peter F. (1955) *The Practice of Management* (reprint, 2004) Elsevier.

Estevadeordal, Antoni; Frantz, Brian & Taylor, Alan M. (2003) "The Rise and Fall of World Trade:1870-1939" *Quarterly Journal of Economics* 118.

Faccio, Maria; Lang, Larry & Young, Leslie (2001) "Dividends and Expropriation" *American Economic Review* 91.

Fradette, Michael & Michaud, Steve (1998) *The Power of Corporate Kinetics* Simon & Schuster.

Fraser, Robin & Hope, Jeremy (2003) *Beyond Budgeting: How Managers Can Break Free from the Annual Performance Trap* Harvard Business School Press.

Fukuyama, Francis (1996) *Trust: the Social Virtues and the Creation of Prosperity* Simon & Schuster.

Gerstner, Louis V. (2002) *Who Says Elephants Can't Dance?* (reprint, 2003) Harper Collins.

Gordon, Andrew (1996) *The Rules of the Game: Jutland and British Naval Command* (reprint, 2005) John Murray.

Gottschalk, Peter (1997) "Inequality, income Growth, and Mobility: The Basic Facts" *Journal of Economic Perspectives* 11(2), Spring.

Gottschalk, Peter & Moffitt, Robert (1994) "The Growth of Earnings Instability in the U.S. Labor Market" *Brookings Papers on Economic Activity.*

Gottschalk, Peter & Smeeding, Timothy (1996) "Cross-National Comparisons of Earnings and Income Inequality" *Journal of Economic Literature*, 35, June.

Goyal, Vidhan Krishan and Park, Chul Won (2001) "Board Leadership Structure and CEO Turnover" *SSRN working paper.*

Gracia, Eduard (2004) "Corporate Short-Term Thinking and the Winner Take All Market" *Business Quest Journal.*

Gracia, Eduard (2005) "The Dangers of Hierarchical Meritocracy: Poor Leadership, Office Politics and the 'Dilbert Principle'" *Magnus Journal of Management*, March.

Gray, John (1998) *False Dawn: The Delusions of Global Capitalism* (reprint, 2002) Granta Books.

Grund, Christian & Westergaard-Nielsen, Niels (2004) "The Dispersion of Employees' Wage Increases and Firm Performance" *IZA Discussion Paper*, 1402.

Handy, Charles (1993) *Understanding Organizations* (fourth edition – reprint, 1999) Penguin.

Handy, Charles (1989) *The Age of Unreason* (reprint, 2002) Random House.

Harris, Marvin (1981) *America Now: The Anthropology of a Changing Culture* (reprint, 1987, under the title *Why Nothing Works: The Anthropolgy of Daily Life*) Simon & Schuster.

Helpman, Elhanan (2004) *The Mystery of Economic Growth* Harvard University Press.

James, Harvey (1999) "Owner as Manager, Extended Horizons and the Family Firm" *International Journal of the Economics of Business*.

James, Sheryl (2003) "Ford Turns 100" *Detroit Free Press*, June 2.

Jennings, Emerson E. (1971) *Routes to the Executive Suite* McGraw-Hill.

Jensen, Michael C. (2000) *A Theory of the Firm: Governance, Residual Claims and Organizational Forms* Harvard University Press.

John, Kose & Ofek, Eli (1995) "Asset Sales and Increases in Focus" *Journal of Financial Economics* 37(1)

Kenwood, A.G. & Lougheed, A.L. (1972) *The Growth of the International Economy, 1820-1960* (Spanish Translation, 1973) Editorial Istmo.

Khurana, Rakesh (2002) *Searching for a Corporate Savior: The Irrational Quest for Charismatic CEOs* Princeton University Press.

Lamoreaux, Naomi R.; Raff, Daniel M. G. & Temin, Peter (2003) "Beyond Markets and Hierarchies: Toward a New Synthesis of American Business History."
*American Historical Review* 108, April.

Lang, Larry H. & Stulz, René M. (1994) "Tobin's q, Corporate Diversification and Firm Performance" *Journal of Political Economy* 102(6).

Lasch, Christopher (1979) *The Culture of Narcissism* (reprint, 1991) W.W. Norton.

Leibenstein, Harvey (1966) "Allocative Efficiency vs. 'X-Efficiency'" *American Economic Review 56*.

Leibenstein, Harvey (1987) *Inside the Firm: The Inefficiencies of Hierarchy* (reprint, 2000) Harvard University Press.

Levy, Frank & Richard J. Murnane (1992), "U.S. Earnings Level and Earnings inequality: A Review of Recent Trends and Proposed Explanations" *Journal of Economic Literature*, September.

Li, Mingfang & Simerly, Roy L. (2000) "Environmental Dynamism, Capital Structure and Performance: A Theoretical Integration and Empirical Test" *Strategic Management Journal.*

Lucier, Chuck; Schuyt, Rob & Spiegel, Eric (2003) "CEO Succession 2002: Deliver or Depart" *Strategy + Business Magazine*, Summer.

Madigan, Charles & O'Shea, James (1997) *Dangerous Company* Penguin Books.

Merton, Robert C. (1990) *Continuous-Time Finance* (reprint, 2001) Blackwell.

Milgrom, Paul & Roberts, John (1992) *Economics, Organization & Management* Prentice Hall.

Murphy, Kevin J. (1998) "Executive Compensation" *SSRN working paper.*

Norwich, John J. (1982) *A History of Venice* (reprint. 2003) Penguin.

O'Reilly, Charles A.; Pollock, Tim & Wade, James (1996) "Overpaid CEO's and Underpaid Managers: Equity and Executive Compensation" *Stamford Research Paper*, 1410.

O'Rourke, Kevin & Williamson, Jeffrey G. (1999) *Globalization and History: The Evolution of a Nineteenth Century Atlantic Economy* MIT Press.

Peters, Thomas J. & Waterman, Robert H. (1982) *In Search of Excellence: Lessons from America's Best Run Companies* (reprint, 2004) Profile Books.

Peyer, Urs & Shivdasani, Anil (2001) "Why Debt Can Hurt Corporate Growth?" *Sloan Management Review, MIT,* Spring.

Politkovskaya, Anna (2004) *Putin's Russia* The Harvill Press, Random House.

Poterba, James M. & Summers, Lawrence H. (1995) "A CEO Survey of U.S. Companies' Time Horizons and Hurdle Rates" *Sloan Management Review*, Fall.

Pryor, Frederic L. (2001) "Will Most of Us be Working for Giant Enterprises by 2028?" *Journal of Economic Behavior and Organization.*

Rajan, Raghuram G. & Wulf, Julie (2003) "The Flattening Firm: Evidence from Panel Data on the Changing Nature of Corporate Hierarchies" *SSRN working paper.*

Revell, Janice (2003) "Mo' Money, Fewer Problems: Is It a Good Idea to Get Rid of the $1 Million CEO Pay Ceiling?" *Fortune Magazine*, March 31.

Ridley, Matt (1998) *The Origins of Virtue* Penguin.

Riesman, David, with Denney, Reuel & Glazer, Nathan (1950) *The Lonely Crowd: A Study of the Changing American Culture* (abridged version, reprint, 2001) Yale University Press.

Rubinstein, William D. (1981) *Men of Property: The Very Wealthy in Britain since the Industrial Revolution* Croom Helm.

Saul, S. Berrick (1986) "Industrialisation: The British Case" published in D. S. Landes et al. *The Industrial Revolution* (Spanish translation, 1988) Editorial Crítica.

Sennett, Richard (1998) *The Corruption of Character: The Personal Consequences of Work in the New Capitalism* (reprint, 1999) W.W. Norton.

Servaes, Henri (1996) "The Value of Diversification During the Conglomerate Merger Wave" *Journal of Finance* 51(4).

Servan-Schreiber, Jean-Jacques (1967) *Le Défi Américain* Denoël.

Snower, Dennis J. (1999) "Causes of Changing Earnings Inequality" *IZA Discussion Paper 29*, January.

Stiglitz, Joseph E. (2002) *Globalization and Its Discontents* Penguin.

Thomas, Gordon & Morgan-Witts, Max (1979) *The Day the Bubble Burst* (Spanish Translation from English, 1986) Orbis.

Williamson, Oliver E. (1998) *The Economic Institutions of Capitalism* Macmillan.

Womack, James P.; Jones, Daniel T. & Roos, Daniel (1991) *The Machine that Changed the World: the Story of Lean Production* Harper.

Whyte, William H. (1956) *The Organization Man* (reprint, 2002), University of Pennsylvania Press.

# INDEX

# NOTES

[1] Plautus' original Latin maxim is, as it is well known, *"homo homini lupus"*.

[2] See for example Snower (1999) or Jensen (2000).

[3] Adams (1996).

[4] This waste is often referred to in economic literature as "X-inefficiency", thus using the term Harvey Leibenstein proposed for them in a pioneering article (Leibenstein, 1966). While measuring this inefficiency is obviously very difficult, there is a whole body of research devoted specifically to this subject –for a good reference book on this topic, see for example Jensen (1999).

[5] Jensen (2000).

[6] Sennett (1998).

[7] Bauman (2000).

[8] *"Risikogesellschaft"* - Beck (1992).

[9] Servan-Schreiber (1967).

[10] See for example Levy & Murmane (1992), Gottschalk & Smeeding (1997) or Atkinson (2003).

[11] Gotschalk (1997).

[12] Snower (1999).

[13] Gottschalk & Moffitt (1994), also cited by Snower (1999).

[14] Rajan & Wulf (2003).

[15] Murphy (1998).

[16] Revell (2003).

[17] Quoted by Sennett (1998).

[18] Harris (1981); the book has been reprinted in subsequent editions under the title *Why Nothing Works: The Anthropology of Daily Life.*

[19] Fukuyama (1996).

[20] Jennings (1971), as quoted by Lasch (1979).

[21] Whyte (1956).

[22] Quoted in Fradette & Michaud (1998).

[23] Khurana (2002).

[24] Lucier, Schuyt & Spiegel (2003).

[25] Bodily & Brunner (2002).

[26] Quoted by Birkinshaw (2003).

[27] Sennett (1998).

[28] Riesman (1950).

[29] Behind this basic conclusion of neoclassical economic theory there are a number of more restrictive, technical assumptions −for a rigorous analytical development see, for example, Merton (1990) or Campbell & Viceira (2002). For the purposes of the argument presented in this chapter, however, we do not need to dive any deeper into these technicalities.

[30] Indeed, of the "big ten" studios that dominate today's Hollywood cinema industry, seven were founded before 1925, the year the first non-silent movie, "The Jazz Singer", was released. These include Paramount (founded in 1912), Universal (also 1912), 20th Century Fox (1915), Columbia (1920), Warner Bros. (1923), Disney (1924) and Metro Goldwyn Mayer, which was born in 1924 as a merger between three older studios founded in 1916 (Metropolitan Pictures), 1917 (Samuel Goldwyn Pictures) and 1918 (Louis B. Mayer Pictures).

[31] There is a wealth of (often highly formalised) literature in economics dealing with the problem of when does free, unregulated market exchange lead to an "optimum" and when it is preferable to group producers in an organisation whose internal mechanisms are not governed by internal prices but by a central command structure –i.e., a firm. Indeed, we could trace back the theory behind this at least to Ronald Coase's famous 1937 article *The Nature of the Firm*. It would go well beyond the aims of this book, however, to attempt to discuss any of these works explicitly. For our purposes, suffice here to say that the statements in the main text are consistent with the results of this branch of economic literature.

[32] For a layman's exposition see for example Ridley (1998).

[33] Lawrence & Lorsch (1967) – as quoted by Peters & Waterman (1982).

[34] Drucker (1955).

[35] Jensen (2000).

[36] For this summary of the M&S case I rely primarily on Bevan (2001).

[37] Chandler (1977).

[38] Thomas & Max-Witts (1979).

---

[39] Donkin (2001).

[40] Chandler (1990).

[41] Drucker (1955).

[42] As quoted in James (2003).

[43] Chandler (1990).

[44] Norwich (1982).

[45] Kenwood & Lougheed (1972).

[46] This paradox of the relatively small accumulated wealth and short-lived heritage of most of the industrialists that led the First Industrial Revolution has already been highlighted, for example, in Rubinstein (1981) –as quoted by Saul (1986).

[47] Chandler (1990).

[48] This interpretation is fully consistent with modern agency theory. In particular, the idea that industrial concentration is due to the impact of information asymmetries (i.e., like in the prisoner's dilemma) on an integrated process has already been put forward, for example, by Williamson (1998) or, most recently, by Lamoreux, Raff & Temin (2003).

[49] O'Rourke & Williamson (1999), as quoted in Helpman (2004).

[50] Estevadeordal, Frantz & Taylor (2003), as quoted in Helpman (2004). The historical values these authors estimate for the global ratio of imports + exports divided by total GDP are: 1800 (2%); 1870 (10%); 1900 (17%); 1913 (21%); 1929 (14%); 1938 (8%); 1950 (14%); 1973 (23%); 1992 (27%). I take 1815 (the year of Waterloo) as the date for the start of the

19th Century globalisation wave because international trade did not really take off until the end of the Napoleonic Wars.

[51] O'Shea & Madigan (1997).

[52] Chandler (1990).

[53] See both Chandler (1990) and Drucker (1955).

[54] Riesman (1950) and Whyte (1956).

[55] Whyte (1956).

[56] Fukuyama (1996).

[57] Chandler (1990).

[58] Although Peter Drucker was also a contemporary of these authors, and despite the fact that he was not altogether unsympathetic to their ideas, I feel his theories were too subtle and complex to fit squarely in this school of thought.

[59] Whyte (1956).

[60] Estevadeordal, Frantz & Taylor (2003), as quoted in Helpman (2004).

[61] Chandler (1990).

[62] Pryor (2001).

[63] Peters & Waterman (1982).

[64] Pryor (2001).

---

[65] Jensen (2000).

[66] Handy (1989).

[67] Berger & Ofek (1995). Similar results have been obtained in other studies such as Lang & Stultz (1994), Comment & Jarrell (1995) or John & Ofek (1995).

[68] Servaes (1996).

[69] Berger & Ofek (1995).

[70] Gerstner (2002).

[71] Jensen (2000).

[72] The interpretation of the IBM turnaround presented in this chapter essentially follows the one in Gerstner's own account (Gerstner, 2002).

[73] Anderson & Reeb (2003).

[74] See for example James (1999) in addition to Anderson & Reeb (2003).

75 Faccio, Lang & Young (2001).

76 Comanor & Miyao (1985), as cited in Leibenstein (1987). Leibenstein also points out that, although Japanese companies tended to rely more on suppliers than their local counterparts, and therefore a larger portion of their gross output value would be due to purchase costs as opposed to their own value added, but he estimated that this difference would in any event explain less than 10%, thus leaving unchallenged the conclusion that the Japanese management system in the 1980s was more productive than the U.S. one, other things being equal.

[77] Womack, Jones & Roos (1991), as cited in Fukuyama (1996).

[78] Poterba & Summers (1995).

[79] Jensen (2000).

[80] Harris (1981).

[81] Dixon (1976).

[82] Gordon (1996).

[83] Gerstner (2002).

[84] Sennett (1998).

[85] Quoted in Handy (1993).

[86] Sennett (1998).

[87] This is a fairly standard result of the efficiency wage theory. A standard exposition of this theory can be found in manuals like Milgrom & Roberts (1992).

[88] Rajan & Wulf (2003).

[89] According to Handy (1993), Urwick stated categorically in 1956 that no manager should supervise the work of more than six subordinates whose work interlocks. Drucker (1954) made a very similar observation, although he was a bit less prescriptive by talking about "six to eight" direct reports as the maximum humanly manageable. One should not need to go back to literature to identify this limit, though: any experienced manager will confirm that managing a flat team of more than six or seven direct reports all too

easily turns into a nightmare where one ends up running up and down like a headless chicken without really getting anything done. The fundamental reason is that a manager always needs to have the spare capacity to deal with an emergency without dropping everything else, but with so many reports chances are that this time buffer does not exist. Under these conditions, the first crisis at one area tends to lead the manager to lose sight of the other areas under his/her supervision, which makes it more likely that another crisis pop up and grow at one or more of these other areas, which diverts the manager's attention even from the remaining areas and at the same time leads him/her to turn into a fire fighter and look for a "quick fix" for each problem instead of a proper solution –which, in turn, means that the issue is more likely to reappear shortly. This is why more predictable environments actually allow larger numbers of direct reports.

[90] Rajan & Wulf (2003).

[91] Goyal & Park (2001).

[92] Rajan & Wulf (2003).

[93] Rajan & Wulf (2003).

[94] Drucker (1954).

[95] See for example O'Reilly, Pollock & Wade (1996), or Grund & Westergaard-Nielsen (2004).

[96] Bebchuck & Grinstein (2005).

[97] Handy (1993).

[98] See for example Li & Simerly (2000) or Peyer & Shivdasani (2001).

[99] Li & Simerly (2000).

[100] Sensibly enough, one of Gerstner's very first significant decisions at IBM was to cut mainframe prices in order to regain market share.

[101] Bodily & Brunner (2002).

[102] Boselie, Hesselink & van der Wiele (2001).

[103] Fraser & Hope (2003).

[104] One could not seriously state that a system where governments' expenditure represents around a 50% of the GDP, as it is the case today in nearly all the developed countries in the OCDE, is, economically speaking, extremely "liberal". The brand of capitalism that dominated Britain's or North America's first industrialisation, for instance, was in many aspects much more liberal than any of our modern developed societies.

[105] Pryor (2001).

[106] There is a lot of recent literature on this subject, so I will just mention a couple of books: Politkovskaya (2004) for a journalistic account of the impact of corruption and misery on modern Russian society, and Stiglitz (2002) for a very critical account of the role of the International Monetary Fund on the liberalisation programme.